really pull th
(They never me

✓ 11. INT. LA

Penny and Dr

✓ "PENNY CHEE

Song ends
he/

R. HORRIBLE'S S
/29/08

ACT ONE

✓ 1. INT. DR.

Dr. Horribl

✓ 2. INT. D
   INT.

✓ "FREEZ
Music
in La
just

TOP
SECRET

E.L.E.

Evil League of Evil

HOMINES NON BONI SERIOSE

TOP
SECRET

Dr. Horrible's
Sing-Along Blog
The Book

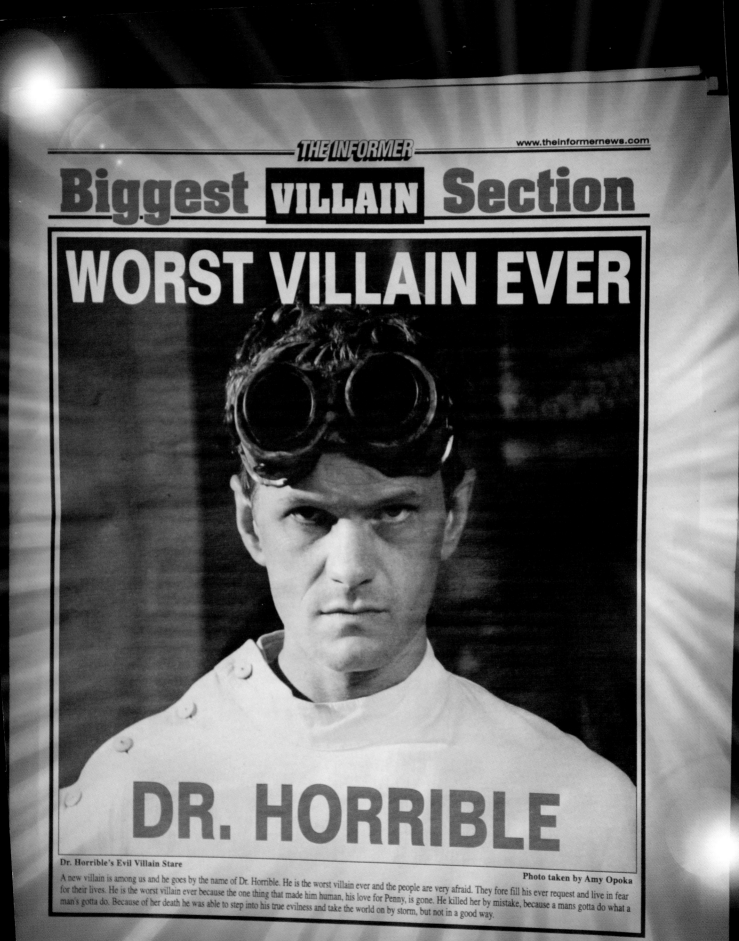

THE INFORMER

www.theinformernews.com

Biggest VILLAIN Section

WORST VILLAIN EVER

DR. HORRIBLE

Dr. Horrible's Evil Villain Stare

Photo taken by Amy Opoka

A new villain is among us and he goes by the name of Dr. Horrible. He is the worst villain ever and the people are very afraid. They fore fill his ever request and live in fear for their lives. He is the worst villain ever because the one thing that made him human, his love for Penny, is gone. He killed her by mistake, because a mans gotta do what a man's gotta do. Because of her death he was able to step into his true evilness and take the world on by storm, but not in a good way.

DR. HORRIBLE'S
SING-ALONG BLOG
THE BOOK

FEATURING THE SCRIPT AND SONGS BY

JOSS WHEDON
MAURISSA TANCHAROEN
JED WHEDON
ZACK WHEDON

WITH CONTRIBUTIONS FROM THE CAST AND CREW

SHEET MUSIC NOTATION BY JANE WATKINS

TITAN BOOKS

DR. HORRIBLE'S
SING-ALONG BLOG
THE BOOK

ISBN 9781848568624

Published by
Titan Books
A division of
Titan Publishing Group Ltd
144 Southwark St
London
SE1 0UP

First edition March 2011
10 9 8 7 6 5 4 3 2

Book designed by Martin Stiff.
Production by Bob Kelly.

Dr. Horrible's Sing-Along Blog unit photography by Amy Opoka.
www.amyopokaphotography.com
Cityscapes and images on pages 8, 50, 70, 71, 80 and 81
© Shutterstock. Used with permission.

Visit our website: www.titanbooks.com

Did you enjoy this book? We love to hear from our readers. Please e-mail
us at: readerfeedback@titanemail.com or write to Reader Feedback at the
above address.

Acknowledgements
The publishers would like to thank the entire cast and crew of Dr.
Horrible's Sing-Along Blog for their co-operation and contributions.
Thanks also go to Nicki Maron at Mutant Enemy for coordinating
everything, and to Abbie Bernstein, Christopher Frankonis (aka The One
True b!X), Beth Nelson at Quantum Mechanix (www.quantummechanix.
com), and Mary Higgins for helping out with photos and interviews.

A CIP catalogue record for this title is available from the British Library.

Printed and bound in China by C&C Offset Printing Co., Ltd.

Contents

INTRODUCTION BY
CAPTAIN HAMMER

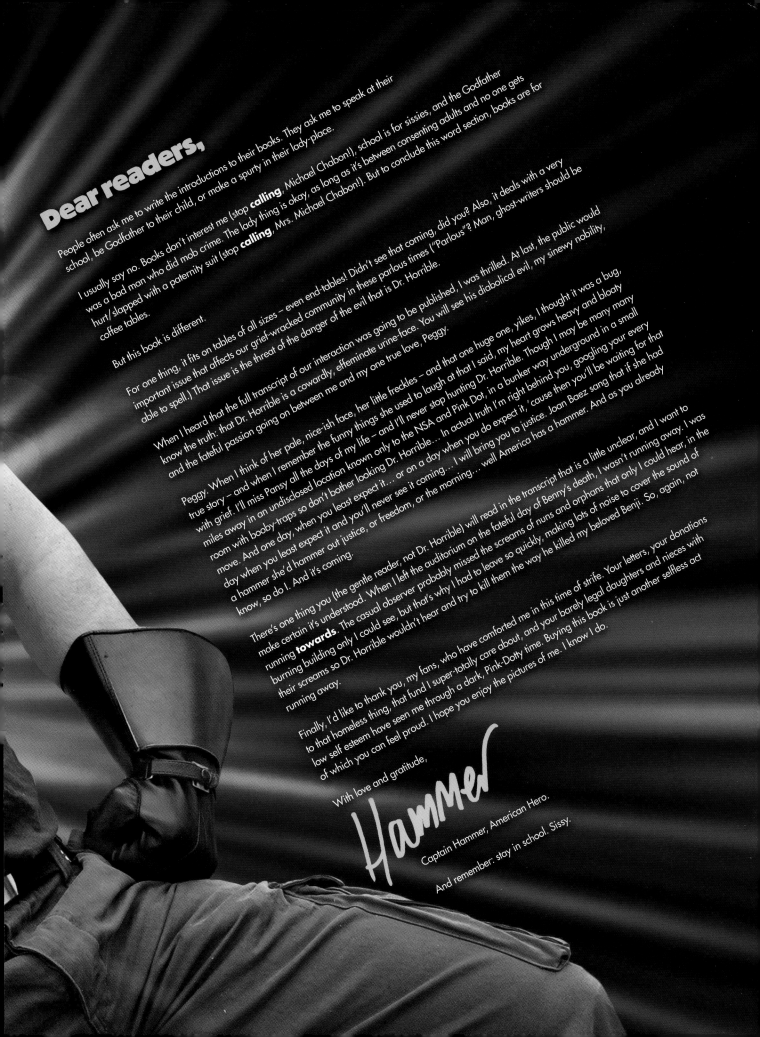

Dear readers,

People often ask me to write the introductions to their books. They ask me to speak at their school, be Godfather to their child, or make a spurty in their lady-place.

I usually say no. Books don't interest me (stop **calling**, Michael Chabon!), school is for sissies, and the Godfather was a bad man who did mob crime. The lady thing is okay, as long as it's between consenting adults and no one gets hurt/slapped with a paternity suit (stop **calling**, Mrs. Michael Chabon!). But to conclude this word section, books are for coffee tables.

But this book is different.

For one thing, it fits on tables of all sizes – even end-tables! Didn't see that coming, did you? Also, it deals with a very important issue that affects our grief-wracked community in these parlous times ("Parlous"? Man, ghost-writers should be able to spell.) That issue is the threat of the danger of the evil that is Dr. Horrible.

When I heard that the full transcript of our interaction was going to be published, I was thrilled. At last, the public would know the truth: that Dr. Horrible is a cowardly, effeminate urine-face. You will see his diabolical evil, my sinewy nobility, and the fateful passion going on between me and my one true love, Peggy.

Peggy. When I think of her pale, nice-ish face, her little freckles – and that one huge one, yikes, I thought it was a bug, with grief. I'll miss Pansy all the days of my life – and when I remember the funny things she used to laugh at that I said, my heart grows heavy and bloaty miles away in an undisclosed location known only to the NSA and Pink Dot, in a bunker way underground in a small room with booby-traps so don't bother looking Dr. Horrible... or on a day when you do expect it, 'cause then you'll be waiting for that move. And one day, when you least expect it... or on a day when you least expect it and you'll never see it coming... I will bring you to justice. Joan Baez sang that if she had a hammer she'd hammer out justice, or freedom, or the morning... well America has a hammer. And as you already know, so do I. And it's coming.

There's one thing you (the gentle reader, not Dr. Horrible) will read in the transcript that is a little unclear, and I want to make certain it's understood. When I left the auditorium on the fateful day of Benny's death, I wasn't running away. I was running **towards**. The casual observer probably missed the screams of nuns and orphans that only I could hear, in the burning building only I could see, but that's why I had to leave so quickly, making lots of noise to cover the sound of their screams so Dr. Horrible wouldn't hear and try to kill them the way he killed my beloved Benji. So, again, not running away.

Finally, I'd like to thank you, my fans, who have comforted me in this time of strife. Your letters, your donations to that homeless thing, that fund I super-totally care about, and your barely legal daughters and nieces with low self esteem have seen me through a dark, Pink-Dotty time. Buying this book is just another selfless act of which you can feel proud. I hope you enjoy the pictures of me. I know I do.

With love and gratitude,

Hammer

Captain Hammer, American Hero.

And remember: stay in school. Sissy.

ORIGIN STORY
A Dr. Horrible Round Table

Jed: The first thing that I remember of any of this was when Zack and I were doing commentary at our apartment for our home movies....

Joss: Oh really?

Jed: Yes.

Joss: Wait, for the ones we made as kids?

Jed: Yes, because you [Joss] used to direct Zack and me in movies when we were children. Some parodies, some original-ish.

Joss: They were all genre parodies. *Stupidman* was clearly a parody of *Gone with the Wind* but then after *Stupidman*, they got less specific. The western, Noir, whatever class I was taking in school at Wesleyan you guys had to suffer through.

Jed: We did *Creature from the Planet Hell*.

Zack: Which was *Aliens*.

Maurissa: You did a war movie too?

Joss: We did *Back to 'Nam*, a documentary about war movies.

Jed: By someone who didn't know anything about the Vietnam War, played by Joss.

Joss: All the roles I play must be hidden from the world.

Jed: I smell a DVD extra...

Joss: I smell a lawsuit!

Joss: So, sixteen years later...

Jed: So you were there and said, "I'm thinking about doing this leettle theeng..."

Joss: I sound like that actually. I sound like Cheech.

Jed: ... and somehow out of that we discerned the words Dr. Horrible.

Maurissa: But your original idea was for it to be a podcast, so when did it morph into the web idea?

Joss: I went through this intense period of songwriting after 'Once More With Feeling' and I loved it, and then I just sort of stopped. The kids came, couldn't make a lot of noise, plus kid-raising. So I thought, I would really love to write songs. I would love to do a podcast, something that resembled a diary but in song. But I have no handle. [sings] "I almost ate carrots, but then I had chocolate..."

Jed: [sings] "I would like to write a song but I can't make noise because there are kids."

Joss: Yes, so then I sort of thought of Dr. Horrible as a little avatar of me, and it would be really fun to have a low-rent super villain trying to get his villainy off the ground. And just can't quite get it done. And make it his weekly blog about his trials and have it all be in song. There were three songs that I was actually working on – the first was 'My Freeze Ray', which I got about half done and then 'When You're My Slave', which was a love song that I threw out. And there was another about Batman – he never says the name but it's Batman – coming and beating him up... this was before we had Captain Hammer... which was quite operatic, apocalyptic, sort of 'Epiphany' type song. Very discordant and very frustrated. That was fun in my head for a few months, but it went nowhere. Maybe more, maybe a year. And then, the writers all got together and said, we have got to go on strike. And I said, this is my opportunity.

Jed: And we started hanging out more on the line.

Joss: I remember seeing you guys at the rally.

Jed: With our red shirts.

Left to right: These early story breakdowns lay the groundwork for the script.

ACT ONE

Podcast

Laundry - MY FREEZE RAY

Moist/Letter - BHC ONE
            intent to pull job

The Job - DOC/HAMMER/PENNY
            Penny
            Crime
            Hammer
            "He saved you?"

ACT TWO

Various - MY EYES
            Spying on dates
            Laundry Buddies

BHC TWO

Laundromat
            Hammer to Billy "Gonna fuck Penny good."

I HAVE TO KILL/SOMEONE'S GOTTA DIE

ACT THREE

Lair - UNTIL THE WORLD IS MINE

TBD - BAD BOYS

EVERYTHING YOU EVER

1/20/08
DR. H

EPISODE ONE

1. Quick Theme.

2. Web-Cam - Showing the newspaper, the cover of which celebrates Captain Handsome's latest victory and laments the latest stomping by Bad Horse. Horrible's latest bad deed only got a brief mention on page seven. He'll never get Penny to notice him. Begins to sing FREEZE RAY --

Continues FREEZE-RAY at laundromat --

3. FREEZE-RAY ends back in front of the web-cam

4. Moist enters with a rejection letter from the league of evil. Doctor Horrible tells Moist he is going to get the final ingredient for his Freeze-Ray tonight.

5. Doctor Horrible staking out some building where someone or some delivery vehicle is going to arrive with a shipment of Bananatonium.

Penny happens by and recognizes him from the laundromat. She has noticed him finally!

Here comes the truck/man with briefcase. He has to start the heist. Horrible excuses himself while he ducks behind a dumpster to don his cape and goggles.

Horrible tries to steal the van using a remote control. -3 part run

Captain Handsome comes to the rescue and starts to sing at some point.

He stops the van, kicks DH ass and gives Penny the impression that he rescued her. Horrible looks on in horror.

assembly of remote a sng

H starts song/
Hammer take c me / Penny thank for saving life

Joss: You guys were making funny videos. [Into tape recorder] Check them out on YouTube. But not the porn one.

Maurissa: No, the porn one has been erased... You know when we first made those videos I did not anticipate anyone watching them besides our friends and family, maybe fifty max.

Joss: The porn one is gone right?

Jed: I want to put it back up.

Maurissa: I'm not comfortable.

Joss: And there was the one you did with Zack and Nick Towne about the WGA, which was priceless. I saw those and meanwhile, because it was the strike, I was on the Internet, on every committee, meeting with tons of people who didn't know what they were doing, and then people from those meetings would come together and form radical splinter groups of people who didn't know what they were doing.

Jed: You are talking about actually producing?

Joss: Writers were talking about producing things for the Internet. Like the guys from *The Office* can just fart genius. They were already doing web episodes. They are funny performers and their stuff is dope. There was other stuff out there I liked...

Jed: But you are talking about people organizing to subvert the networks?

This page: Pre-production, including Joss doing the Dance of Joy (right).

Joss: Yes, they said, "All we need is 100 million dollars and we can make cop shows for the Internet!" And I'm nodding and smiling and thinking, "Well, no…" The things that I had seen that really mattered to me were *The Guild*, Felicia's thing… because it was very home-made but it had production values and she knew how to make it work, and *The Office* stuff, and especially the *Star Trek* episode I saw from *New Voyages*. Just an enormous amount of work, and streamed beautifully for over an hour, I loved the episode but I was also blown away by the amount of work and the quality of the tech that went into streaming this thing. So it made me think, I can do anything! Then, a bunch of us tried to go up to Silicon Valley and say, "Give us money you entrepreneurs you, and we shall create cheap products that can be associated with your companies." I pitched a few things they liked, *Dr. Horrible* being the one I knew no one would get, which they didn't. But they were fired up. They said, "This is great, let's spend three years working out contracts!" World's most timid mavericks, I swear. The only way to do it was by myself and by "by myself" I mean with the help of everyone I know – but funded by me. I know Jed is a dope songwriter, and I have some actor friends… It was a weird thing for me: it was a very meaningful thing, politically, but at the same time, it was a lark. What was our catch-phrase?

Maurissa: "It's an Internet musical!"

Joss: Exactly.

Maurissa: It was our excuse for everything!

Joss: So then we talked about doing it. I was afraid, it was family and it was collaborating with new people. The first thing I remember is getting together at the Montana office. And I think I had finished 'Freeze Ray'.

Maurissa: You played 'Freeze Ray' for us.

Joss: *So* nervous. I just remember banging out a song, maybe our second meeting, and then you and Jed had that pristine demo of 'I Cannot Believe My Eyes', and I just said, "I'd like to withdraw my song…"

Maurissa: And Ben Edlund was also there.

Joss: Ben had been with me on the lines a lot, and there was a point where he said, you *have* to do this. Like he actually gave me the shove to do it. He said, "I have so many super hero puns and I have no use for them! You can't leave me behind."

Maurissa: Yes, he came to a few meetings but then he had to drop out.

Zack: He gave us Moist.

Joss: And he'd been pitching Bad Horse for years on *Angel*, so I hadda have it.

FLASHBACK: Captain Hammer kicking Horrible's ass over and again.

laundromat theatrical Silly Things to differentiate it - Humorous shots - Santa

DR. HORRIBLE (CONT'D)
All the time that you beat me
unconscious I forgive
All the crimes incomplete - listen,
honestly I'll live
Mr. Cool, Mr. Right, Mr. Know-It-
All is through
Now the future's so bright and I
owe it all to you
Who showed me the light → *INT LAB - NIGHT Waits @ Hammer*

It's a brand new me
I got no remorse
Now the water's rising
But I know the course
I'm gonna shock the world
Gonna show Bad Horse
It's a brand new day *INT LAUNDROMAT - smoke fantasy version*

And Penny will see the evil me
Not a joke, not a dork, not a
failure
And she may cry but her tears will
dry
When I hand her the keys to a shiny
new Australia

A CHORUS sings and dances behind him.

DR. HORRIBLE (CONT'D)
It's a brand new day *back to when he's following them*
Yeah the sun is high *BIG GIANT ? IN TRENCH and FAN SQUASH CAMERA*
All the angels sing
Because you're gonna die *or ROOFTOP ?*
Go ahead and laugh
Yeah I'm a funny guy
Tell everyone goodbye...
It's a Brand new day

<u>END ACT TWO</u>

Above:
The read through.
Left and right:
Script rewrites.

Maurissa: And he came up with great songs too.

Joss: Yeah, he has a great voice, very different sound.

Jed: The idea of keeping the project small, the fact that all my music was made in my living room, being able to produce the music in full scale, we basically had everything we needed for pre-production...

Zack: I looked through my computer this morning to look for any relics of *Dr. Horrible* and I found a file called *Mr. Horrible* which is clearly what I thought the title should be... It never occurred to me that Joss probably had an idea of what it should be... and also not realizing that a freeze ray stops time instead of freezing things.

Maurissa: We only had three meetings and then the script was done. Maybe over the course of three weeks?

Joss: Yep. It took about a month to write everything. We broke it down on the white board, and we already knew which songs we

INT. LAUNDROMAT/DR HORRIBLE'S LAB - DAY
PENNY (CONT'D) *Record This* DR. HORRIBLE
There's no happy endings There's no happy endings
So they say So they say
~~Maybe life is sending~~ Not for me anyway *Stop pretending*
~~No a chance to build~~ a brand ~~Maybe life is sending~~ *Stared ish*
new day ~~Take~~ Me a chance to build a brand *Take*
Should I stop pretending new day
OR is This a brand new day

EXT. STREET - DAY *action - LABEL "DEATH RAY"*

Groupie 2 holds up a laminated slip of paper.

HAMMER GROUPIE 2
This is his dry cleaning bill

BOTH GROUPIES
Four sweater vests

NEW SHELTER LOBBY
INT. ~~AUDITORIUM~~ - NIGHT *~~REST BANNER~~ w/ SHELTER CARING HANDS*

Press, groupies and homeless people mill about the room. *statue*
Penny is seated on stage beside a podium. A lumpy, unhappy
man, MAYOR HANKINS, steps up to the podium and people begin
to take their seats. He clears his throat and taps the mic.

MAYOR
Hello. Hello everyone, thank you
all for coming. We are very
pleased to be here tonight. The *trim mayor*
building we're gathered in was
going to be levelled until my *indicate Hammer*
attention was turned to the efforts *statue ~~statue for me~~*
of the Caring Hands Homeless *across the*
Shelter, an organization which has *hill*
been doing good in this city for
quite some time. The man
responsible for enlightening me
needs no introduction but he
insisted so...

He clears his throat and reads from a note card.

MAYOR (CONT'D)
"He keeps us safe while we're
sleeping at night. He strikes fear
in the hearts of men that would
choose a life of crime.
(MORE)

were going to use. And knowing the end of Act One was going to be Billy, interrupted by Hammer... I remember the first meeting thinking, let's kill Penny!

Jed: Yeah, I remember hearing Zack saying, "I think this should be sad." And I think what you meant is that he should be sort of pathetic, and then Joss is like, "Let's kill Penny!" And I said, "We should be *that* sad!"

Zack: Yes, I referenced *Extras* as a model of sadness.

Maurissa: So then we had the script, and then a demo of all of the songs.

Joss: But Zack, you had written songs before but didn't write any songs this time.

Zack: Yes, I wrote a song once.

Joss: It was beautiful! You did it *a cappella* on stage.

Zack: I just have not written a song since and the thought of writing another is sort of intimidating.

Joss: And Maurissa, you also play and compose?

Maurissa: Yes, I play... and there are two songs that are original and I feel like are okay to the ears.

Jed: Maurissa is really good at improvising with songs. Like the horns, with the Neil stuff. Basically what riding in the car with us is: I'm stuck at the stoplight and she does the side kick thing, harmonies, riffs...

Joss: Kai and I do the same thing. She sings and I back her up. Maybe less professional than you two. So we had the talent going, the will...

Zack: ... the free time that unemployed people have...

Joss: ... but having the Jed factory and finding a line producer were the two things that kept me from going insane.

Maurissa: The Jed factory, producing the music and all the Internet stuff: really couldn't have done it without you.

Joss: Absolutely.

Maurissa: [to Jed] Want to get married?

Joss: Now onto how we came up with Dr. Horrible. We had the basic premise of Dr. Horrible and his cold gun...

Jed: The thing I love most about it is the simplicity of that first act: he gets what he wants, but introduces his nemesis to his girlfriend... The hardest part was the heist with the van – that was the thing I really didn't know if it would work.

Joss: Yeah, that sequence was horrible and not in the Internet success way, in the old-fashioned way, just the logistics of the heist, and then coming to Universal for one day, one big shoot, the stunts, the lighting...

Jed: At the last script reading, we still didn't understand the heist. But we got the characters.

Joss: The villain thing just felt so right to me because I think villains are super poignant, and I don't trust heroes, which is why I had trouble making *Angel* for five years. Tall, handsome people who do good bother me.

Maurissa: I remember we were talking about Penny: she needs to be something more than just a girl. She should have a cause, some interest.

Joss: I was thinking some environmental thing and then you [Maurissa] said, "She should do something for the homeless." And I looked at you and said "Why?", and you said, "Because it's hilarious!" I thought you were some kind of monster. Really,

I was appalled. And then I couldn't stop running with the homeless jokes... and honestly, I think some of the best lyrics I've ever written are in 'Everyone's a Hero'.

Maurissa: "He smells like poo..."

Jed: ... and that was an important turning point because she really pushed hard for her idea.

Joss: We got Penny not to be generic, but she doesn't operate on the same level as the supers. Even in the final product, she doesn't have a Penny catch phrase, doesn't have all the big lines, she's delightful and Felicia brings a lot to it, but she's the girl in the picture.

Jed: Her and Nathan that is.

Zack: She *is* fighting "the man"... it's her cause that brings up Billy's thing about putting power in people's hands.

Joss: People are always saying, does Dr. Horrible reflect the politics of the strike?

Zack: I'm gonna say yes, but I have no idea, but I would like it to, because it means I'm a thoughtful person.

Jed: No one is going to buy that.

Joss: It wasn't on purpose, but I realize that I come back to that theme, "There are giant corporations that are trying to destroy people" all the time, and I've worked in Hollywood for twenty-two years – there can't be any kind of connection.

Jed: Yes, and Dr. Horrible had to have a reason why he was evil.

Joss: He had to be the hero. The world is not balanced and the person who thinks that the best way for things to get better is for things to be destroyed and then rebuilt, I mean I feel that more and more every time when I open the newspaper.

Jed: And the other thing that makes this idea work is the idea of the hero being the good-looking, strong guy and the thing you don't like about heroes is what Captain Hammer embodies. He's a huge dick! He has muscles and dresses up in costumes.

Zack: Especially when he doesn't have a nerdy alter ego.

Joss: There's no Clark Kent.

Jed: One of the best things about *Dr. Horrible* for me was doing it the same way as we had done our stupid shit. Like all the records I've made, all the home videos, we are editing and making it ourselves, just with bigger toys and bigger actors. Bigger than we'd even expected.

Joss: Exactly, at first you mentioned Zack playing Dr. Horrible and Maurissa as Penny.

Joss: Yes, Neil fought so hard for that part, we had like thirty guys and he was last.

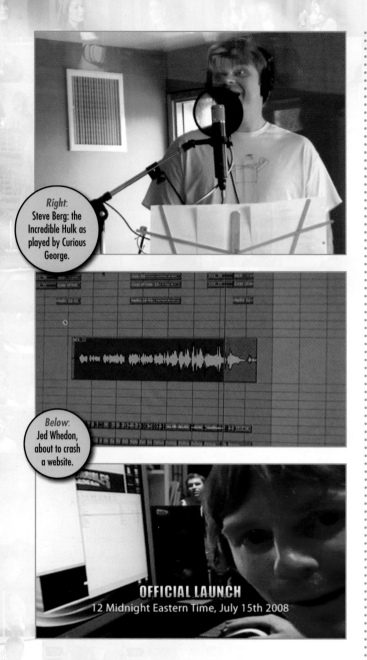

Right:
Steve Berg: the Incredible Hulk as played by Curious George.

Below:
Jed Whedon, about to crash a website.

OFFICIAL LAUNCH
12 Midnight Eastern Time, July 15th 2008

Maurissa: We didn't even know if he had a voice.

Joss: Yes he was terrible, but he had a spark and I thought, I could mold him. And through editing, we made him look really passable. Actually, I was too scared to ask him. I was too scared to ask Nathan.

Maurissa: Who was your first call?

Joss: I believe it was Neil. But then they both said yes so fast! I tried to talk them out of it, but it didn't work.

Maurissa: He had wanted to work with you for a while?

Joss: That's my version! So then, both guys said yes and then Felicia, because of *The Guild* Christmas thing that she made for a hundred dollars, it was very clear that she could sing (and that

no one else in her cast could). I remember thinking, she just has Penny energy. She has Penergy.

Jed: We didn't know her, but we thought, "Fuck this idea. Who?"

Maurissa: Yeah, we didn't know her at all then.

Joss: Classic Felicia – she's like, "I don't know, you should have me read. I had four years of opera training, but I'm not sure I can pull it off." She's hardcore nerdsmart – that great arrogant insecurity. The first time I met her on *Buffy*, she told me she double majored in math and violin and I said, "I don't know your name yet!"

Maurissa: And then Simon, who was a buddy of ours. I think Simon was not the prototype you had envisioned for Moist?

Joss: Well, my thing about Moist was that I wanted him to be completely at ease with his moisture. So I was kind of tugging on him during the shoot. He was hilarious, and so sweet, and at the end of it he asked me, "Did I just do the exact opposite of what you wanted?" But Moist is so him, I loved what he brought.

Jed: The other thing I remember is when we were casting the groupies: we had cast you [Maurissa] and Stacey as the groupies, and then you [Joss] suggested a third groupie, "A guy, maybe he's gay – hey Jed, maybe you should do it?"

Joss: I don't think I would have said that if I said maybe... But I thought you put in the third because you said it would be much prettier with a third part harmony.

Jed: Yes, but there was also the Steve component. He's 6' 3", big and blond and has a lisp.

Joss: Basically he's the Hulk as played by Curious George.

Jed: He's hilarious and a huge *Buffy* fan. You don't know this, but the first day we recorded, he was outside Rob's house an hour early! He was so excited. And as he drove away, he rolled down his window and started screaming!

Zack: So that was the casting, then the first read through.

Joss: In my living room.

Jed: And then [producer] David Burns was there... and we realized it was real.

Maurissa: Getting that horse...

Joss: Yes, give it up to Dobber... he did not poo on set.

Maurissa: He looked right at camera when asked to.

Joss: More than I can say for Nathan...

Jed: But I remember that read through. Everybody getting together... except Nathan, Neil and Simon. They all forgot. And Felicia showed up early with pastries – and tonsillitis!

Joss: That sent a chill, the boys not showing. 'Cause by this time, the strike had ended, and there was a little bit of hesitation... I had *Dollhouse*... Neil was back in production, everyone was back in production... whereas Nathan was just sitting around thinking, "I'm so cool..."

Jed: "Should I get another mirror? I think so."

Joss: So then Nathan bolted over from the Valley and Neil, we heard from several hours later.

Jed: He'd been working, but he was mortified. "I really want to do it, please don't cut me."

Joss: He meant it literally because I carry a razor.

Jed: And you said, "Jed, you have to read his part," and I was not okay with that.

Maurissa: You were great! Let's get married.

Joss: You did really well... but my salient memory from the read through, even though we had scripts, Nathan insisted reading from his iPhone!

Zack: The same phone that would one day be Dr. Horrible's van controlling machine!

Joss: Was it really the same phone?

Zack: I have no idea. I know Nathan got his buddy to design the controls and put it up on a site... I was just trying to find an out, wrap this shit up! Shut up! I hate you!

Jed: Well, I don't think we'll do better than that.

Maurissa: No one's gonna hear this, right?

ACT ONE

INT. DR. HORRIBLE'S LAB - DAY

WEBCAM VIEW: DR. HORRIBLE laughs an evil, maniacal laugh into the camera. He wears a lab coat and goggles that rest on his forehead. The lab is cluttered with various scientific equipment, schematics, disassembled electronic devices, and some dirty clothes.

DR. HORRIBLE

AH-ha-ha-ha-ha-ha!!! Ah-HAH-ha-haha-ha...
(pause)
So that's, you know, coming along... I'm working with a vocal coach, strengthening the...
(indicates stomach)
Lotta guys ignore the laugh. And that's about standards. You don't get into the Evil League of Evil without a memorable laugh.
You think Bad Horse didn't work on his whinny?
(fearful reverie)
His terrible death-whinny...
(recovers)
No response BTW from the League yet, but my application is strong this year, letter of condemnation from the Deputy Mayor, that's gotta have weight, so, fingers crossed... Emails! 2sly4U writes:
(holds up printout)
"Hey, genius," Wow, sarcasm! That's original...
(a beat as he realizes he said that sarcastically)
Uh, "Where are the gold bars you were supposed to pull out of

that bank vault with your Transmatter Ray? Obviously it failed or it would be in the papers." Well, no, they're not gonna say anything to the press, but...
(smiles)
Behold. Transported from there...
(holds up a plastic bag of brown paste)
...to here! The molecules tend to...shift during the transmatter, uh, event...but these came through in bar shape and were clearly...and it's not about making money, it's about **taking** money. Destroying the status quo, because the status is...**not** quo. This world is a mess and I just need to rule it. I'm gonna --
(puts bag daintily far away)
-- smells like cumin...
(holds up more printouts)
So transmatter is 75% and more importantly, the **Freeze Ray** is almost up. This is the one. Stops time. Freeze Ray. Heard it here first.
(holds up another printout, grimaces)
Oh. Great. Our old friend Johnny Snow: Doctor Horrible, I see you are once again afraid to do battle with your nemesis. I waited at Dooley Park for 45 minutes --" Okay. Dude. You're not. My nemesis. My nemesis is Captain Hammer.

ANGLE: PICTURE OF CAPTAIN HAMMER. Resume:

DR. HORRIBLE (CONT'D)
Captain Hammer? Corporate tool, dislocated my shoulder -- again -- last week... I'm trying to change the world, okay? I don't have time for a grudge match with every poser in a parka. Besides, **kids** play in that park. Hmmm,
(hasn't read this one)
DeadNotSleeping writes, "Long time watcher first time etc...
(skips ahead)
...You always say in your blog that you will show her the way, show her you are a true villain. Who is 'her' and does she even know that you're..."

He falls silent, mouthing the beginning of a response, then just thinking.

MUSIC CUE -- "MY FREEZE RAY" intro

Above:
Joss Whedon's original lyric sheet for 'My Freeze Ray'.

INT. LAUNDROMAT/DR. HORRIBLE'S LAB - DAY

As the music continues, we see Dr. Horrible (in street clothes) (obviously the same guy but goes by the name, BILLY) entering with a bunch of laundry. He stops, seeing:

ANGLE: DR. HORRIBLE'S POV --

PENNY. Clearly the girl. Bookishly pretty, in her own space, sitting by her machine reading "The Toy Collector".

Alternating between versions: one where he actually sings and she can't hear, one where he's just going through his routine and not singing, one where he actually talks and she responds, one where he's actually freezing things and being awesome, and one singing in front of his webcam.

> DR. HORRIBLE
> *Laundry day*
> *See you there*
> *Under things*
> *Tumbling*

Wanna say
Love your hair
Here I go
Mumbling
With my freeze ray I will stop the world
With my freeze ray I will
find the time to find the words to
Tell you how
How you make
Make me feel
What's the phrase?
Like a fool
Kinda sick
Special needs
Anyways
With my freeze ray I will stop the pain
It's not a death ray or an ice beam
That's all Johnny Snow
I just think you need time to know
That I'm the guy to make it real
The feelings you don't dare to feel
I'll bend the world to our will

And we'll make time stand still
That's the plan
Rule the world
You and me
Any day
(to Penny)
Love your hair

PENNY
What?

DR. HORRIBLE
No - I just...love the... air...

DR. HORRIBLE (CONT'D)
Anyway
With my freeze ray I will stop

INT. DR. HORRIBLE'S LAB - CONTINUOUS

Cradling his Freeze Ray, he finishes the song -- and MOIST
enters, holding mail. (No longer webcam view.)

MOIST
Hey Doc.

DR. HORRIBLE
(stows his ray awkwardly)
Moist! My evil moisture... buddy. What's going on?

MOIST
Life a' crime. Got your mail.

Dr. Horrible takes the mail, which leaves a long snail trail of
icky moisture on it. He leafs through it.

DR. HORRIBLE
Hey, didn't you have a date last night? Conflict Diamond told
me you two were doubling with Bait and Switch.

MOIST
Yeah...

DR. HORRIBLE
(prodding)
Yeah...?

MOIST
It was all right... I kinda thought I was supposed to end up with
Bait, but...

DR. HORRIBLE
I hear ya. I saw Penny today.

MOIST
You talk to her?

DR. HORRIBLE
So close. I'm just a few weeks away from making a
real, audible connection, I just...
(looking at a letter)
Oh my God.

MOIST
Is that from the League?

DR. HORRIBLE
It's from **him**. That's his seal, right?

MOIST
The leader? The... oh my God.

DR. HORRIBLE
I got a letter from Bad Horse.

MOIST
That's so hardcore. Bad Horse is legend.
He rules the League with an iron hoof. Are
you sure you wanna --

But Doc tears the letter open. As he opens it:

MUSIC CUE -- "BAD HORSE CHORUS I"

The BAD HORSE CHORUS, a trio of jolly, evil cowboys in mustachios and Stetsons, pop their heads into frame (two on the left and one on the right), singing --

> BAD HORSE CHORUS
> *Bad Horse, Bad Horse*
> *Bad Horse, Bad Horse*
> *He rides across the nation, the thoroughbred of sin*
> *He got the application that you just sent in*
> *It needs evaluation, so let the games begin*
> *A heinous crime, a show of force*
> *(A murder would be nice of course)*
>
> *Bad Horse, Bad Horse*
> *Bad Horse, he's bad*
> *The evil league of evil is watching so beware*
> *The grade that you receive'll be your last, we swear*
> *So make the bad horse gleeful, or he'll make you his mare*
> *You're saddled up; there's no recourse*

It's "hi-yo, silver!"
Signed: Bad Horse.

And they're gone.

> MOIST
> It's not a no...

> DR. HORRIBLE
> Are you kidding? This is great! I'm about to pull a **major** heist. The wonderflonium I need for my Freeze Ray? It's being transported tomorrow.

> MOIST
> Armored car?

> DR. HORRIBLE
> Courier van. Candy from a baby.

> MOIST
> You need anything... dampened, or made soggy?

> DR. HORRIBLE
> Thanks, but... the League is watching. I gotta go it alone.

EXT. STREET - DAY

ON PENNY - she hands out flyers to passersby.

MUSIC CUE -- "PENNY'S SONG (CARING HANDS)"

> PENNY
> *Will you lend a caring hand*
> *To shelter those who need it*
> *Only have to sign your name*
> *Don't even have to read it*
>
> *Would you help... No? How about you?*

ANGLE - DR. HORRIBLE in a back alley entrance. He holds a small duffle-bag and peers around the corner with binoculars--

POV - DR. HORRIBLE

A white van pulls up outside a building down the street. The driver gets out and runs inside.

RESUME - DR. HORRIBLE

He drops the duffle and removes a little silver electronic device from inside. He looks both ways and then hucks the device in the van's direction. It flies, seemingly magnetically

drawn to the van's top where it attaches itself. Dr. Horrible pulls a remote control from the bag and flips it on --

ANGLE - VAN

The electronic device on the top of the van lights up --

RESUME - DR. HORRIBLE

He works the remote control's touchscreen --

ANGLE - VAN

As the engine revs --

RESUME - DR. HORRIBLE

Pleased the device is working, he smiles. Penny suddenly appears behind him --

> PENNY (CONT'D)
> (sings)
> *Will you lend a --*
>
> DR. HORRIBLE
> (spinning)
> AHH!

DR. HORRIBLE'S REMOTE CONTROL

THE NIFTY IPHONE REMOTE CONTROL PANEL WAS CREATED BY NATHAN FILLION'S FRIEND P. J. HAARSMA, THE AWARD-WINNING AUTHOR OF THE SOFTWIRE BOOKS.

How did you first become involved in *Dr Horrible's Sing-Along Blog*?

Nathan called me one night and asked me if I could make a "thing" that would work on his iPhone. He was vague and I really didn't understand what he was doing. He mentioned something about a remote, Joss, and a musical. I remember thinking, "I hope you're not singing."

Did you meet with Joss Whedon and the rest of the team or was the design done remotely?

Nathan and I did this ourselves. We went back and forth together on the design a few times. I don't have an iPhone so I would call Nathan to keep testing it out. I tried to make it as interactive as possible. All I knew was that someone was going to push a button to make a van move. When Nathan showed Joss he loved it. He just wanted the GAS and BRAKE buttons to be bigger.

Did you visit the set to see your remote control in action?

Again no. Remember, I'm the guy who didn't see *Firefly* until just last year. The whole process was very informal. My friend called and asked for help and I did my best for him. Next thing I know I hear servers are crashing from his project. I'm just glad to have been a part of it. After Nathan announced [the online version of the remote] at Comic-Con, over 28,000 people clicked on the Softwire link in just 24 hours.

Get your own remote here:
http://thesoftwire.com/horrible_remote.html

P. J. Haarsma's charity Kids Need To Read:
www.kidsneedtoread.org

(P. J. Haarsma interviewed by Mary Higgins, aka WorldofHiglet, for Whedonage.com)

9:42 AM

Horrible Van Remote

DISCONNECTED

LIGHTS   RADIO
HORN   WIPERS

BRAKE   GAS

PENNY
Ooh!

DR. HORRIBLE
(oh my god, it's Penny)
Ahhh. Hah. What?

PENNY
I was wondering if I could.... Hey, I know you.

DR. HORRIBLE
Hello. You know me? Cool. I mean, yeah. You do. Do you?

PENNY
From the laundromat.

DR. HORRIBLE
(nodding)
Wednesdays and Saturdays except twice last month you skipped the weekend or, if that was you, it could be someone else, I mean I've **seen** you, Billy, is my name.

PENNY
I'm Penny.
(re: his control)
What are you doing?

DR. HORRIBLE
Texting. It's important or I'd stop. What are **you** doing?

She looks at her clipboard, puts on her big smile --

PENNY
Actually, I'm out here volunteering for the Caring Hands Homeless Shelter. Can you spare a minute?

Dr. Horrible peers over his shoulder --

POV - DR. HORRIBLE

The van is idling outside the building --

RESUME - DR. HORRIBLE

Reluctantly --

DR. HORRIBLE
Okay, go.

PENNY
Okay. We're hoping to open up a new location soon, expand our efforts. There's a great building nearby that the city's just going to demolish and turn into a parking lot. If we get enough signatures --

DR. HORRIBLE
(disparagingly)
Signatures.

PENNY
Yeah.

DR. HORRIBLE
I'm sorry, go on.

PENNY
I was saying maybe we could get the city to donate the building to our cause. We'd be able to provide two hundred and fifty new beds, get people off the streets and into job-training...

Doc's attention has wandered to the van --

PENNY (CONT'D)
... so they can buy rocket packs and go to the moon and become florists, you're not really interested in the homeless, are you?

DR. HORRIBLE
(turning back)
I am. But they're a symptom; you're treating a symptom and the disease rages on, consumes the human race while you're

getting signatures. The fish rots from the head as they say so my thinking is why not cut off the head.

PENNY
Of the human race?

DR. HORRIBLE
It's not a perfect metaphor but I'm talking about an overhaul of the system. Putting the power in...different hands.

PENNY
I'm all for that...
(beat)
This petition is about the building.

DR. HORRIBLE
I'd love to sign.

PENNY
Thank you.

He does --

DR. HORRIBLE
I'm sorry, I come on strong.

25

PENNY
But you signed.

DR. HORRIBLE
Well, I can't turn my back on a fellow... laundry... person --

PENNY
If **we** can't stick togeth --

A beeping from his controller makes him spin around, turning his back on her instantly.

ANGLE: THE VAN. The courier opens the back door and puts in a metal briefcase marked: WONDERFLONIUM (And in smaller letters: DO NOT BOUNCE).

Doc is all concentration. Penny looks like she's trying not to look hurt.

PENNY (CONT'D)
I'll probably see you there.

She moves off and he works the controller. Turns back too late with a feeble --

DR. HORRIBLE
Yeah I will, I'll --

He deflates as he realizes he's blown his first meeting with her. Penny is already down the street a bit, intercepting a couple.

MUSIC CUE -- "A MAN'S GOTTA DO"

DR. HORRIBLE (CONT'D)
She talked to me. Why did she talk to me **now**?
(torn)
Maybe I should...

But he can't.

DR. HORRIBLE (CONT'D)
A man's gotta do what a man's gotta do
Don't plan the plan if you can't follow through

Doc ducks back into the alley and emerges a second later in full costume --

DR. HORRIBLE (CONT'D)
All that matters: taking matters into your own hands

He works the remote --

ANGLE - THE DRIVERLESS VAN takes off, the driver just opening the door to get in --

DRIVER
Stop! Hey!

DR. HORRIBLE
Soon I'll control everything, my wish is your command --

ANGLE - CAPTAIN HAMMER drops right on top of the van from a mighty leap that we did not film.

CAPTAIN HAMMER
Stand back everyone,
nothing here to see
Just imminent danger, in the middle of it, me

Yes, Captain Hammer's here, hair blowing in the breeze

He kneels to look at the device.

CAPTAIN HAMMER (CONT'D)
And the day needs my saving expertise

-- and he punches it, crushing it onto the hood like a bug, sparks flying.

CAPTAIN HAMMER (CONT'D)
A man's gotta do what a man's gotta do

ANGLE - DR. HORRIBLE

CRUNCH!

THE DAY NEEDS MY SAVING EXPERTISE

Shaking the remote, he realizes
he is no longer in control --

CAPTAIN HAMMER (CONT'D)
Seems destiny ends with me saving you

ANGLE - VAN

The Captain jumps off and smiles at a stunned FEMALE
BYSTANDER as the van runs wild in the BG.

ANGLE - DR. HORRIBLE

Watching in horror --

POV - DR. HORRIBLE

Penny, in the direct path of the runaway van --

RESUME - DR. HORRIBLE

He struggles with his remote --

CLOSE ON - Him hitting a window that says "BRAKES"

CAPTAIN HAMMER (CONT'D)
The only doom that's looming is you loving me to death

ANGLE - PENNY

Looks up at the van approaching as Hammer whips into
frame and palms her ten feet into a pile of garbage bags.

CAPTAIN HAMMER (CONT'D)
So I'll give you a sec to catch your breath

ANGLE - THE BROKEN DEVICE

It lights up.

ANGLE - THE BRAKE PEDAL

Goes down without a foot on it.

ANGLE - VAN

It stops inches from Hammer's outstretched hand.
Doc, meanwhile, runs up --

DR. HORRIBLE
You idiot!

CAPTAIN HAMMER
Doctor Horrible. I should have known you were behind this.

DR. HORRIBLE
You almost killed her!

CAPTAIN HAMMER
I remember it differently.

DR. HORRIBLE
(looking past him)
Is she --

Captain Hammer grabs him by the neck, choking the next
word out of him.

CAPTAIN HAMMER
It's curtains for you, Horrible. Lacy, gently wafting curtains.

DR. HORRIBLE
(WTF?)
Mmmf?

The garbage moves and Penny starts
struggling her way free, singing:

PENNY
(in shock)
Thank you Hammer man, I don't think I can
Explain how important it was that you stopped the van

Captain Hammer begins pummeling Doc with his free hand, slams Horrible's face into the grill of the van a couple of times to the beat, then tosses him away as the girl approaches.

PENNY (CONT'D)
I would be splattered I'd be crushed under debris
Thank you sir for saving me

CAPTAIN HAMMER
Don't worry about it.

A man's gotta do what a man's gotta do
Seems destiny ends with me saving you

ANGLE - DR. HORRIBLE

He rises with some difficulty and slinks away behind the van to the rear door. He pulls a tiny lock-disabling device from his pocket and places it on the door which pops open momentarily.

As he retrieves the Wonderflonium, through the windshield he can see, with despair, the connection between the girl of his dreams and the man of his nightmares.

This page:
Filming Captain Hammer pushing Penny and 'stopping' the van.

CAPTAIN HAMMER
*When you're the best, you can't
rest, what's the use
There's ass needs kicking, some
ticking bomb to diffuse
The only doom that's looming
is you loving me to death*

PENNY
*You came from above
I wonder what you're Captain of
My heart is beating like a drum
Must be, must be in shock
Assuming I'm not loving you
to death*

DR. HORRIBLE
(over their singing)
*Are you kidding?
What heist were you watching?
Stop looking at her like that
Did you notice that he threw you in the garbage?
I stopped the van, the remote control was in my hand
Whatever*

CAPTAIN HAMMER/PENNY
So please give me a sec to catch my breath

Doc grabs it and limps off as, in the background, we see
Captain Hammer charming Penny.

DR. HORRIBLE
Balls.

END ACT ONE

30

A Horrible Experience
by Felicia Day

My Dr. Horrible experience began with a very brief email:

"How well do you sing? -j"

That's "-j" for Joss Whedon. Needless to say I answered, "YES!" because when Joss asks you to do something, you'd be an idiot not to do it!

Reflecting back on the production, something I don't think people realize is how truly grass roots it was. From recording the songs in one short afternoon at Joss's house, to Jed creating the posters, banner art and website, to Neil clomping his shoes against the wall for sound effects as we recorded "Commentary: The Musical" for the DVD. No advertising was spent on the show. I used clothes out of my own closet. But the end result was the most epic web series ever created, and that's because of an emotion that infused every step of the process: Pure joy.

It was so clear when I read the script for the first time that Jed, Joss, Maurissa and Zack had written something simply for the pleasure of creating it. It came through in the soaring lyrics of the songs. No one in Hollywood would have greenlit a "Superhero Musical", it would have been insane to even pitch it. But they didn't need permission, they just WROTE. And that feeling carried through to the physical production. There was an infectious spirit on the set that felt like we were kids 'putting on a show.' No other set I've been on has been infused with that kind of joy. I hope to experience something like it again, but I bet I never will. It was magic.

XOXO

Felicia

HERE'S A STORY OF A GIRL

ACT TWO

INT. DR. HORRIBLE'S LAB - DAY

WEBCAM VIEW: Dr. Horrible stares at the camera, his face a map of frustration and pain. He shakes his head --

MUSIC CUE -- "MY EYES"

CUT TO:

EXT. CITY STREETS - NIGHT

Dr. Horrible is out and about in the city, observing the people around him.

> DR. HORRIBLE
> *Any dolt with half a brain*
> *Can see that humankind has gone insane*
> *To the point where I don't know*
> *If I'd upset the status quo*
> *If I threw poison in the water main*

He comes up to a building and looks in the window.

> DR. HORRIBLE (CONT'D)
> *Listen close to everybody's heart*
> *And hear that breaking sound*
> *Hopes and dreams are shattering apart*
> *And crashing to the ground*

INT. RESTAURANT - NIGHT

DOC'S POV - Hammer and Penny are leaning close, having an intimate dinner, laughing...

> DR. HORRIBLE
> *I cannot believe my eyes*
> *How the world's filled with filth and lies*
> *But it's plain to see*

CLOSE ON - DOC outside, looking grim.

> DR. HORRIBLE (CONT'D)
> *Evil inside of me is on the rise*

INT. RESTAURANT - NIGHT

Penny and Captain Hammer continue dinner by candlelight. REVEAL they're inside...

INT. CARING HANDS SOUP KITCHEN - NIGHT

Penny and Captain Hammer are surrounded by HOMELESS PEOPLE as they eat their dinner. Captain Hammer isn't thrilled, but he's hiding it from her.

> PENNY
> (re: a Homeless Man)
> *Look around*
> *We're living with the lost and found*
> *Just when you feel you've almost drowned*
> *You find yourself on solid ground*
> *And you believe*
>
> *There's good in everybody's heart*
> *Keep it safe and sound*
> *With hope, you can do your part*
> *To turn a life around*

Hammer turns to talk to a FAN. We notice Dr. Horrible in a "moustache disguise" in the BG, serving soup.

Above:
Dr Horrible's
'moustache disguise'
is applied.

PENNY (CONT'D)
I cannot believe my eyes
Is the world finally growing wise
'Cause it seems to me
Some kind of harmony
Is on the rise

EXT. MACARTHUR PARK – DAY

Penny and Captain Hammer sit on a bench eating frozen yogurt. Hammer is secretly disgusted by the pigeons that flutter near their feet. Doc lurks in the bushes nearby.

CAPTAIN HAMMER
When you're the best, you can't rest, what's the use
There's ass needs kicking, some ticking bomb to diffuse
The only doom that's looming is you loving me to death

PENNY
You came from above
I wonder what you're Captain of
My heart is beating like a drum
Must be, must be in shock
Assuming I'm not loving you to death

EXT. MACARTHUR PARK LAKE – DAY

Captain Hammer is in a pedal boat, pedaling in circles at superhuman speed. Penny smiles and waves to him from the grass as Doc watches from a bridge behind.

DR. HORRIBLE
Listen close to everybody's heart
And hear that breaking sound
Hopes and dreams are shattering apart
And crashing to the ground

PENNY
There's good in everybody's heart
Keep it safe and sound
With hope, you can do your part
To turn a life around

INT./EXT. SHELTER – NIGHT

Doc and Penny back up against opposite sides of the wall, her inside with the warm light, him outside with the cold dark, and both sing in close profile:

THERE'S ASS NEEDS KICKING

any dolt with half a brain
can see humankind gone insane
to the point where I don't know
if I'll upset the status quo
when I throw poison in the water main

Listen close to everybody's heart
and hear that breaking sound
I'll tear the mother f-ing earth apart
crashing to the ground

I cannot believe my eyes
How the worlds filled with filth and lies
but it's plain to see
evil inside of me is on the rise

soaring like a plane
it's as clear as the sky is after rain
he's is stronger than a train
and he's treating me sweet as sugar cane

There's good in everybody's heart
so safe and sound
with hope, you can do your part
turn the world around

I cannot believe my eyes
every day holds a new surprise
but it's plain to see
rapture inside of me is on the rise

Left:
An early draft of the lyrics for 'My Eyes'.

DR. HORRIBLE
I cannot believe my eyes
How the world's filled with filth
and lies
But it's plain to see
Evil inside of me is on the rise

PENNY
I cannot believe my eyes
How the world's finally
growing wise
And it's plain to see
Rapture inside of me is on the
rise

He moves out of his frame as Hammer comes into her frame, laying a smooch on her.

INT. LAUNDROMAT - DAY

Billy and Penny load their dirties into neighboring washing machines --

PENNY
-- so dumb that we've been coming here so long and never spoke.

BILLY
I know. All those months doing this stunningly boring chore --

PENNY
I'm a fan of laundry.

BILLY
-- Psych! I love it.

PENNY
The smell of fabric softener. The feel of warm clothes in your hands...

He's opening a bag from the yogurt place...

BILLY
It's so good... Hey this is weird. I order one frozen yogurt and they give me two. You don't like frozen yogurt do you?

PENNY
I love it.

BILLY
You're kidding, what a crazy random happenstance. Well, here.

He hands the Fro-Yo to Penny --

BILLY (CONT'D)
How was your weekend? Spend the whole time hunting wild signatures?

PENNY
Actually, I went on a date.

BILLY
(smiling through it)
Get right outta town. How was it?

PENNY

Unexpected. He's a really good-looking guy, and I thought he was kind of cheesy at first --

BILLY

Trust your instincts.

PENNY

-- but then he turned out to be totally sweet. Sometimes people are just layered like that. There's something totally different underneath than what's on the surface.

Billy nods, considering the topic --

BILLY

And sometimes there's a third, even deeper level and that one is the same as the top, surface one.

PENNY

Huh?

BILLY

Like with pie. Are you gonna see him again?

PENNY

I think I am.
(beat, concerned)
Billy?

BILLY

Yeah?

PENNY

You're driving the fork into your leg.

He looks --

BILLY

So I am. Hilarious!

CUT TO:

INT. DR. HORRIBLE'S LAB - DAY

WEBCAM VIEW: Doc hoists the Freeze Ray onto his lap. He's starting off pretty cocky --

DR. HORRIBLE

Enough. The wait is over. This, my friends, is my Freeze Ray which, with the addition of the Wonderflonium I obtained at my famously successful heist last week - I say successful in that I achieved my objective, it was less successful in that I inadvertently introduced my arch-nemesis to the girl of my dreams and now he's taking her out on dates and they're probably

gonna french-kiss or something. She called him sweet. How is he sweet?

His eyes fall on the massive Freeze Ray he is holding --

DR. HORRIBLE (CONT'D)

Right! Freeze Ray. So as of tonight I am in the Evil League of Evil if everything goes according to plan, which it will because I hold a PhD in horribleness. See you at the aftermath. Peace!
... But not literally.

The screen goes black --

CUT TO:

INT. DR. HORRIBLE'S LAB - NIGHT

WEBCAM VIEW: Doctor Horrible has a black eye and is a little emotionally fragile at the moment. He clears his throat --

DR. HORRIBLE
The Freeze Ray needs work. I also need to be a little bit more careful about what I say on this blog. Apparently the LAPD and Captain Hammer are among our viewers. They were waiting for me at the Mayor's dedication of the Superhero Memorial Bridge. The Freeze Ray takes a few seconds to warm up and I wasn't... Captain Hammer threw a car at my head. Not to worry, though, because --

His cell phone rings.

DR. HORRIBLE (CONT'D)
One sec.

He opens it and puts it to his head.

DR. HORRIBLE (CONT'D)
Hello?

MUSIC CUE -- "BAD HORSE CHORUS II"

The Bad Horse Chorus pops into frame --

BAD HORSE CHORUS
He saw the operation you tried to pull today
But your humiliation means he still votes "neigh"
And now assassination is just the only way
There will be blood, it might be yours
So go kill someone
Signed: Bad Horse

They disappear. Dr. Horrible stares at the screen --

CUT TO:

INT. DR. HORRIBLE'S LAB - DAY

Moist sits cross-legged on the floor while Doc paces. Moist is shaking his head, he holds an unopened jar of peanut butter in his hands, twisting at its top --

MOIST
Kill someone?

DR. HORRIBLE
Would you do it, to get into the Evil League of Evil?

MOIST

Look at me, man, I'm Moist. At my most badass I make people feel like they want to take a shower. I'm not E.L.E. material.

DR. HORRIBLE

Killing's not elegant or creative. It's not my style.

MOIST

You've got more than enough evil hours to get into the henchman's union.

Horrible waves off the idea --

DR. HORRIBLE

I'm not a henchman. I'm Dr. Horrible. I've got a PhD in horribleness.

MOIST
(beat)
Is that the new catch-phrase?

DR. HORRIBLE

I'm workshopping it. There's others -- I deserve to get in, you know I do... but killing? Really?

MOIST

Hourglass says she knows a kid in Iowa who grows up to become president... that'd be big...

DR. HORRIBLE

I'm not gonna kill a kid! Besides, Hourglass can't really time-travel; they just call her that 'cause she's stacked.

MOIST
Smother an old lady?

DR. HORRIBLE
(appalled)
Do I even know you?

CUT TO:

INT. LAUNDROMAT - DAY

Penny and Billy sit with their yogurt. He's pretty down...

BILLY

I just, you know I really think I'm qualified for this, this job, but I can't get a foot in the door.

PENNY
I'm sure you will...

BILLY

I wanna do great things, you know? I wanna be an achiever, like Bad Horse.

PENNY
(shocked)
The thoroughbred of Sin?

BILLY
I meant Gandhi.

PENNY
I've gotten turned down for plenty of jobs. Even fired a few times.

BILLY
I can't imagine anybody firing you.

PENNY
Neither could I. Now I can visualize it really well. But you know, everything happens --

BILLY
Don't say "for a reason".

PENNY
(busted)
No! Noo, I'm just saying, "everything happens".

BILLY
(down)
Not to me.

MUSIC CUE -- "PENNY'S SONG"

PENNY
Here's a story of a girl
Who grew up lost and lonely
Thinking love was fairytale
And trouble was made only for me

She rises, moves toward the window...

PENNY (CONT'D)
Even in the darkness
Every color can be found
And every day of rain
Brings water flowing
To things growing in the ground

She looks out at the city. He is captivated -- rises, coming closer to her...

PENNY (CONT'D)
Grief replaced with pity
For a city barely coping
Dreams are easy to achieve
If hope is all I'm hoping to be

She turns back to him and they start to get closer than perhaps they'd intended...

> PENNY (CONT'D)
> *Anytime you're hurt there's one*
> *Who has it worse around*
> *And every drop of rain*
> *Will keep you growing*
> *Seeds you're sowing in the ground*

She touches his cheek, lifts his head...

> PENNY (CONT'D)
> *So keep your head up Billy, buddy*

He smiles. She remembers herself, feels compelled to add:

> PENNY (CONT'D)
> It's like Captain Hammer is always saying --

> BILLY
> Right, him. How are things with Cheesy-On-The-Outside?

> PENNY
> Good. They're good. He's nice. I'll be interested to know what you think of him -- he said he might stop by.

There is a sudden panic in Billy --

> BILLY
> Stop by here.

> PENNY
> Yeah.

He checks the time on his bare wrist --

> BILLY
> Wow. Goodness. Look at my wrist. I have to go.

Billy rises and moves for the door --

> PENNY
> What about your clothes?

Billy does a one-eighty, opens up the washer and looks in --

> BILLY
> I don't love these. See ya!

He spins around and walks face first into a wall of man. As he slowly looks up --

> CAPTAIN HAMMER
> Pardon me.

> BILLY
> (frog in throat)
> Pardon.

44

Penny's beside them --

PENNY
Billy this is Captain Hammer.

Hammer's grin is genuine and disarming --

CAPTAIN HAMMER
Billy, the laundry buddy. Well it is **very** nice to meet you.

BILLY
We're meeting now for the first time.

He cocks his head --

CAPTAIN HAMMER
You look horribly familiar...

BILLY
One of those faces I guess.

CAPTAIN HAMMER
Have I seen you at the gym?

BILLY
(of course!)
At the gym!

CAPTAIN HAMMER
(thinking it through)
I don't go to the gym. I'm just naturally like this. Oh well.

He wraps an arm around Penny --

CAPTAIN HAMMER (CONT'D)
Anybody want to know what the Mayor is doing behind closed doors? He's signing a certain building over to the Caring Hands group as a new homeless shelter...

PENNY
Oh my god!

CAPTAIN HAMMER
Apparently the only signature he needed was my fist. But with a pen in it. That I was signing with.

PENNY
I can't believe it.

BILLY
(to Penny, sincerely)
Congratulations.

PENNY
Thank you.
(kisses Hammer)
Thank **you**!

The washer buzzes --

PENNY (CONT'D)
Ooh.

Penny moves away to the machine --

BILLY
Well this is great. I wish I could stay and chit-chat.

Hammer puts a hand on Billy's shoulder --

CAPTAIN HAMMER
Well, hey, it was really nice to meet you, **Doctor**.

He leans in close, shaking his head --

CAPTAIN HAMMER (CONT'D)
You've got a little crush, don't you, Doc? That's gonna make it hard to hear this. Later on I'm going to take little Penny back to my place, show her the command center, the Hammer Cycle, maybe even the Ham-jet... You think she likes me now? I'm gonna give her the night of her life just because you want her. And I get. What you want. Penny's giving it up, giving it up hard 'cause she's with Captain Hammer and **these...**
(holds up his fists)

...are not the Hammer.

He exits frame. Billy cannot move. Hammer re-enters frame, quietly adding --

> CAPTAIN HAMMER (CONT'D)
> The Hammer is my penis.

Captain Hammer puts his arm around Penny as they exit the laundromat.

MUSIC CUE -- "BRAND NEW DAY"

Dr. Horrible's look of shock morphs into an unexpected, fierce smile.

> DR. HORRIBLE
> *This appeared as a moral dilemma 'cause at first*
> *It was weird though I swore to eliminate the worst*
> *Of the plague that devoured humanity it's true*
> *I was vague on the "how" - so how can it be that you*
> *Have shown me the light*

EXT. STREETS - CONTINUOUS

Dr. Horrible exits the laundromat and onto the street. He walks closely behind Captain Hammer and Penny.

> DR. HORRIBLE
> *It's a brand new day*
> *And the sun is high*
> *All the birds are singing*
> *That you're gonna die*
> *How I hesitated*
> *Now I wonder why*
> *It's a brand new day*

FLASHBACKS - Captain Hammer kicking Horrible's ass over and again:

These are done all on the same street corner. 1) Flowers bloom as Doc gets his ass kicked. 2) A MAN, in a Hawaiian shirt and straw hat, watches Hammer and Doc brawl. 3) Hammer throws Doc into a pile of orange/yellow leaves. 4) It lightly snows as Hammer pummels Doc. Santa Claus in the BG.

All this over:

> DR. HORRIBLE (CONT'D)
> *All the time that you beat me unconscious I forgive*
> *All the crimes incomplete - listen, honestly I'll live*
> *Mr. Cool, Mr. Right, Mr. Know-It-All is through*
> *Now the future's so bright and I owe it all to you*
> *Who showed me the light*

INT. DR. HORRIBLE'S LAB – NIGHT

Dr. Horrible throws darts at a photo of Captain Hammer.

> DR. HORRIBLE
> *It's a brand new me*
> *I got no remorse*
> *Now the water's rising*
> *But I know the course*
> *I'm gonna shock the world*
> *Gonna show Bad Horse*
> *It's a brand new day*

He throws himself on the couch, holds a picture of her clearly taken with a long lens from behind a bush or fence....

> DR. HORRIBLE (CONT'D)
> *And Penny will see the evil me*
> *Not a joke, not a dork, not a failure*
> *And she may cry but her tears will dry*
> *When I hand her the keys to a shiny new Australia*

EXT. STREETS – DAY

CLOSE ON Horrible, low angle, the sun on his face -- blissful and sweet.

> DR. HORRIBLE
> *It's a brand new day*
> *Yeah the sun is high*
> *All the angels sing*

PULL BACK TO REVEAL Dr. Horrible is three stories tall, stomping through the streets like a Japanese monster. His labcoat blows in the wind.

> DR. HORRIBLE (CONT'D)
> *Because you're gonna die*
> *Go ahead and laugh*
> *Yeah I'm a funny guy*

DR HORRIBLE'S POV - Looking down on Hammer, alone now.

REVERSE: Dr. Horrible stares down at us, enormous, about to squash us like a bug.

> DR. HORRIBLE (CONT'D)
> *Tell everyone goodbye...*
> *It's a brand new day*

His massive foot fills the frame. BLACK.

END ACT TWO

IT'S A BRAND NEW DAY

A Horrible Memory
by Simon Helberg

So **my first memory** of Dr. Horrible involved a read **through with the cast and writers/producers**. I was sitting in my apartment, **when the phone rang. It was Maurissa** asking where I was and if I had **forgotten about the reading. After an** eruption of sweat, urine and panic, I raced over to **Joss's house for the** reading, only to find that many people had forgotten **about it. It was a match** made in heaven. We proceeded to read through with Jed **reading as Dr. Horrible** and I remember looking over at Nathan and noticing that **he was reading** off his iPhone, **which was** a fairly new invention at the **time. And** I thought, "Wow, that **guy is cool.** That guy is **from** the future."

So another read/sing thru was organized so that **Joss, Jed, Zack** and **Maurissa** could hear Neil and Felicia and Nathan and myself. When Neil and Felicia finished singing 'My Eyes/On the Rise' for the first time, the room was frozen still. We all looked around and I remember **Joss** saying, "I just got a little teary-eyed." **And all the guys in the room kind of** chuckled and mumbled something **like "sissy."**

We then all turned around to wipe **the stream of sissy** tears away from **our faces.**

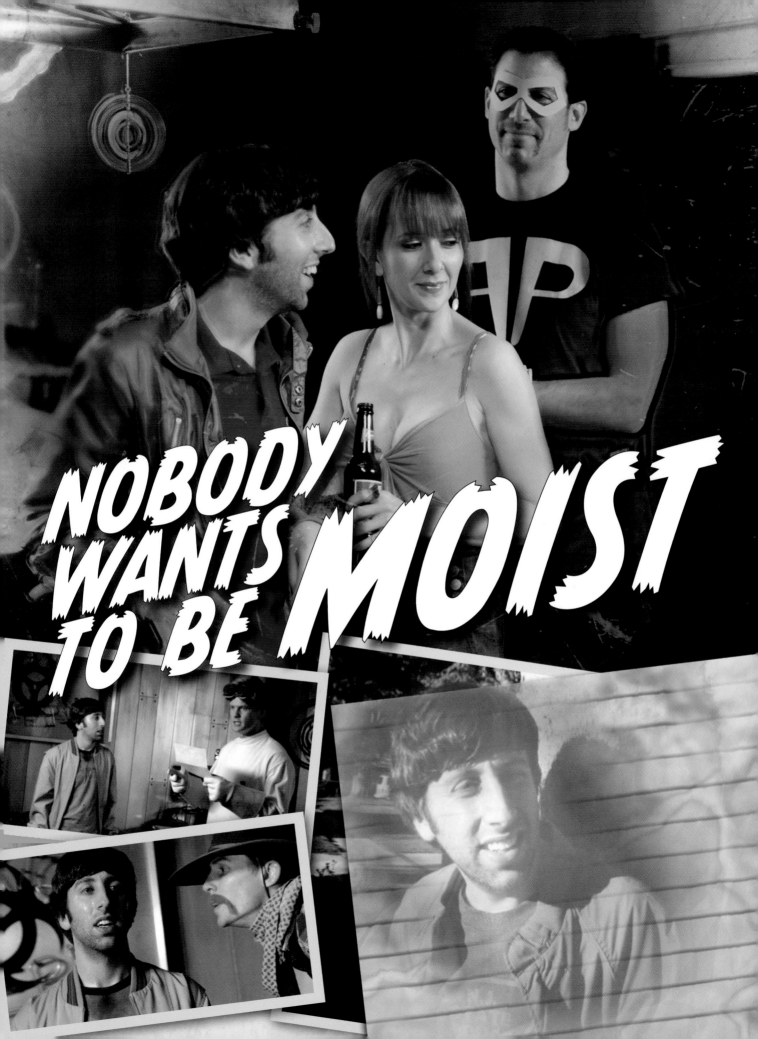

ACT THREE

INT. NEWSROOM - DAY

Two NEWSANCHORS trade banter.

> FEMALE ANCHOR
> Looks like we're learning what a true hero is.

> MALE ANCHOR
> The mayor himself will be on hand to dedicate the new homeless shelter and unveil the statue of Captain Hammer.

> FEMALE ANCHOR
> It's a good day to be homeless.

> MALE ANCHOR
> (laughing)
> It certainly is.

Widen to see we're:

INT. DR. HORRIBLE'S LAB - DAY

MUSIC CUE -- "SO THEY SAY"

We see several cuts of Dr. Horrible hard at work, building, welding, going over equations, working swiftly and furiously on various gadgets in his lab.

Top left:
David Fury and Marti Noxon read the news.
Above:
Rob Reinis and Mike Boretz move.

EXT. STREET - DAY

Two GUYS are unloading equipment from a truck.

> GUY
> *So they say Captain Hammer's become a crusader*
> *Political - He's cleaning up the streets*

> OTHER GUY
> *About time*

EXT. STREET - DAY

Three CAPTAIN HAMMER GROUPIES are standing on the street, addressing camera as though they're being interviewed.

> HAMMER GROUPIE 1
> *So they say that it's real love*

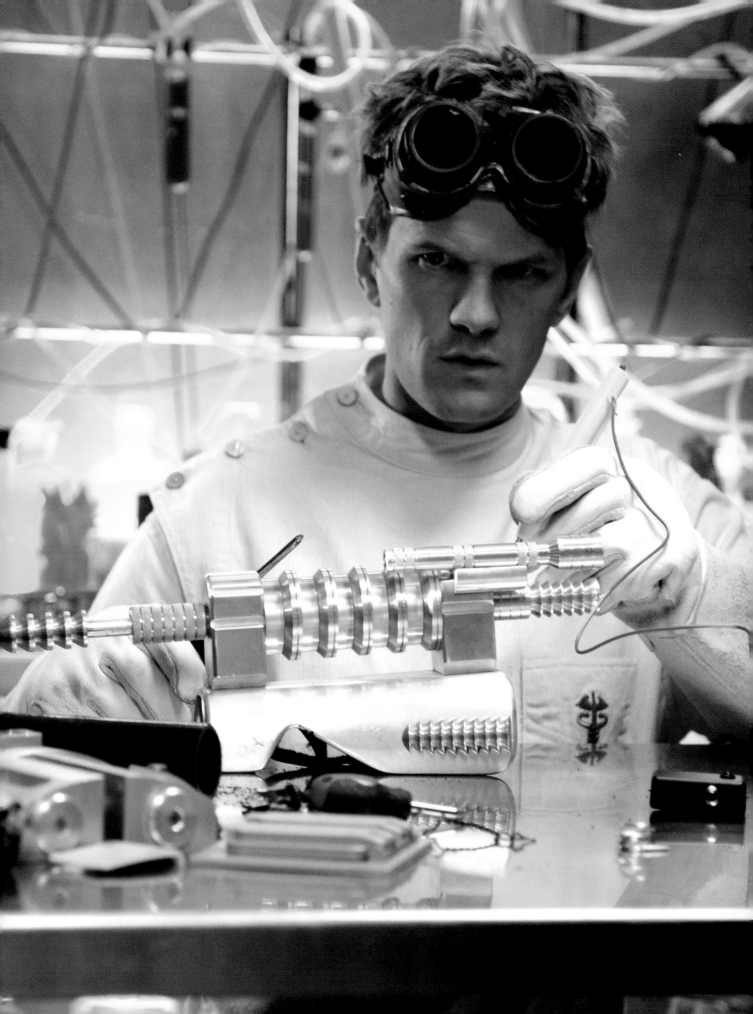

ALL GROUPIES
So romantic

HAMMER GROUPIE 2
(turns to show t-shirt back)
He signed this

INT. NEW SHELTER LOBBY – DAY

It's shabbily grand, and bustling with people bringing in supplies and setting up the room for a big press conference. Penny is approaching Hammer in foreground, stowing her cellphone.

PENNY
So they say we'll have blankets and beds
We can open by Monday
Thanks to you

He takes her close, shaking his head, "No"...

HAMMER
Thanks to me

INT. NEWSROOM – DAY

A MALE AND FEMALE ANCHOR sit. An image of Hammer outside the new shelter on their screen.

NEWSANCHORS
It's the perfect story

NEWSMAN
So they say

NEWSWOMAN
A hero leading the way

BOTH
Hammer's call to glory

NEWSWOMAN
Let's all be our best

NEWSMAN
Next up - Who's gay?

As they finish, we pull back to reveal...

INT. DR. HORRIBLE'S LAB – DAY

He's working working working.

EXT. STREET – DAY

The Groupies:

HAMMER GROUPIE 3
So they say he saved her life

HAMMER GROUPIE 1
*They say she works with the homeless
And doesn't eat meat*

ALL GROUPIES
We have a problem with her

HAMMER GROUPIE 2
(holding up something laminated)
This is his hair

INT. NEW SHELTER LOBBY – DAY

Hammer takes a moment by himself...

HAMMER
This is so nice
I just might sleep with the same girl twice
They say it's better the second time
They say you get to do the weird stuff

The Groupies step into frame in the far BG.

BOTH GROUPIES
We'd do the weird stuff

INT. LAUNDROMAT - DAY

Penny sits by herself. There are two frozen yogurts, but Billy is conspicuously absent.

PENNY
This is perfect for me
So they say
I guess it's pretty okay
After years of stormy
Sailing have I finally found the bay

During the above someone enters and she cranes hopefully for Billy, but it's not him.

INT. APARTMENT - DAY

Moist is holding the phone to his ear. He's with another

VILLAIN, just hanging.

MOIST
He's still not picking up.

INT. LAUNDROMAT/ DR. HORRIBLE'S LAB - DAY

SPLITSCREEN:

PENNY	DR. HORRIBLE
There's no happy ending	*There's no happy ending*
So they say	*So they say*
Should I stop pretending	*Not for me anyway*
Or is this a brand new day	*Stop pretending*
	Take the chance to build a
	brand new day

Dr. Horrible "upgrades" his Stun Ray by putting tape on it labeled "Death" over "stun".

EXT. STREET - DAY

Hammer Groupie 2 holds up a laminated slip of paper.

HAMMER GROUPIE 2
This is his dry cleaning bill

ALL GROUPIES
Four sweater vests

INT. NEW SHELTER LOBBY - NIGHT

PRESS, VOLUNTEERS, HAMMER GROUPIES, and HOMELESS PEOPLE mill about the room. At one end of the room is something large covered in a massive red cloth. At the opposite end Penny is seated on a stage beside a podium. MAYOR HANKINS, steps up to the mic and people begin to take their seats. He clears his throat.

MAYOR
Thank you, thank you everyone. Justice has a name and the name that it has, besides justice, is Captain Hammer.
(looks up)
Ladies and Gentlemen, your hero.

Captain Hammer leaps onto stage, arms extended wide.

CAPTAIN HAMMER
Thank you. Thank you, Mayor, for those kind words.
(reading from cards)
I hate the homeless.
(next card)
-ness that plagues our city. Everyone should have the basic...
(tosses them)
I don't need tiny cue-cards. When I fell deeply in love with my serious long-term girlfriend Penny -- Wave your hand, Penny --

She does, sheepishly. This is a bit much.

CAPTAIN HAMMER (CONT'D)
-- There she is. Cute, right? Sort of a quiet, nerdy thing. Not my usual but nice. Anyway, she got me into this whole homeless thing, which is just terrible, and I've realized that I'm not the only hero in the room tonight. I'm not the only one... who's fighting.

MUSIC CUE -- "EVERYONE'S A HERO"

CAPTAIN HAMMER (CONT'D)
It may not feel too classy
Begging just to eat
But you know who does that? Lassie
And she always gets a treat
So you wonder what your part is
'Cause you're homeless and depressed
But home is where the heart is
So your real home's in your chest

Everyone's a hero in their own way
Everyone's got villains they must face
They're not as cool as mine
But folks, you know it's fine to know your place
Everyone's a hero in their own way
In their own not-that-heroic way

Right:
Joss's original, slightly
different lyrics
for 'Everyone's
A Hero'.

EVERYONE'S A HERO

IT MAY NOT SEEM TOO CLASSY
BEGGING ON THE STREET
BUT YOU KNOW WHO DOES THAT? LASSIE
AND SHE ALWAYS GETS A TREAT
SO YOU WONDER WHAT YOUR PART IS
'CAUSE YOU'RE HOMELESS AND DEPRESSED
BUT HOME IS WHERE THE HEART IS
SO YOUR REAL HOME'S IN YOUR CHEST

EVERYONE'S A HERO IN THEIR OWN WAY
EVERYONE'S GOT VILLAINS THEY MUST FACE
THEY'RE NOT AS COOL AS MINE
BUT LISTEN GUYS IT'S FINE TO KNOW YOUR PLACE
EVERYONE'S A HERO IN THEIR OWN WAY
IN THEIR OWN NOT-THAT-HEROIC WAY

SO I THANK MY GIRLFRIEND, PENNY
(YEAH WE TOTALLY HAD SEX)
SHE SHOWED ME THERE WERE MANY
DIFFERENT MUSCLES I COULD FLEX
THERE'S THE DELTOIDS OF COMPASSION
AND THE ABS OF BEING KIND
IT'S NOT ENOUGH TO BASH IN
HEADS - YOU'VE GOT TO BASH IN MINDS

EVERYONE'S A

I'M POVERTY'S NEW SHERIFF
THE JOHN WAYNE OF THE SLUMS
A HERO DOESN'T CARE IF YOU
YOU'RE A BUNCH OF DRUNKEN BUMS

So I thank my girlfriend, Penny
(Yeah, we totally had sex)
She showed me there's so many
Different muscles I can flex

The Hammer Groupies in the audience swoon.
A mortified Penny slowly edges her way through
the crowd towards the exit.

> CAPTAIN HAMMER (CONT'D)
> *There's the deltoids of compassion*
> *And the abs of being kind*
> *It's not enough to bash in heads*
> *You've got to bash in minds*

He moves into the crowd...

> CAPTAIN HAMMER (CONT'D)
> *Everyone's a hero in their own way*
> *Everyone's got something they can do*
> *Get up, go out and fly*
> *Especially that guy - he smells like poo*
> *Everyone's a hero in their own way*
> *You and you and mostly me and you*
> *I'm poverty's new sheriff*

> *And I'm bashing in the slums*
> *A hero doesn't care*
> *If you're a bunch of scary alcoholic bums*

Everybody!

> CAPTAIN HAMMER (CONT'D)   HAMMER GROUPIES
> *Everyone's a hero in their own*   *We're heroes too*
>   *way*   *We're just like you*
> *Everyone can blaze a hero's trail*
> *Don't worry if it's hard*
> *If you're not a friggin' 'tard you*
>   *will prevail*

Hammer gestures toward the red cloth across the room. As the
red cloth slowly falls away --

CAPTAIN HAMMER (CONT'D)
Everyone's a hero in their own
way
Everyone's a hero in their --

HAMMER GROUPIES
We're heroes too

-- It's no statue. It's DR. HORRIBLE with his tripod-mounted Freeze Ray firing at Captain Hammer. Dr. Horrible lets out his perfected, evil, maniacal laugh. The crowd gasps.

ON CAPTAIN HAMMER - completely frozen.

MUSIC CUE -- "SLIPPING"

Dr. Horrible makes his way up the center aisle of the room and through the crowd. He sings to the frozen Captain -- and then to the people he passes, his Freeze Ray giving off an idle hum.

DR. HORRIBLE
Look at these people - amazing how sheep'll
Show up for the slaughter
No one condemning you - lined up like lemmings
You led to the water
Why can't they see what I see? Why can't they hear the lies?
Maybe the fee's too pricey for them to realize
Your disguise is slipping
I think you're slipping

61

EVERYTHING YOU EVER

HERE LIES EVERYTHING
THE WORLD I WANTED AT MY FEET
MY VICTORY'S COMPLETE
SO HAIL TO THE KING

[EVERYTHING YOU EVER]

ARISE AND SING

~~SO HE~~ SO YOUR WORLD'S BENIGN
SO YOU THINK JUSTICE HAS A VOICE
AND WE ALL HAVE A CHOICE
WELL NOW YOUR WORLD IS MINE

(EVERYTHING YOU EVER)

AND I'M JUST FINE

BRIDGE

NOW THE NIGHTMARE'S REAL
NOW DR HORRIBLE IS HERE
TO MAKE YOU QUAKE WITH FEAR
TO MAKE THE WHOLE WORLD KNEEL

[EVERYTHING YOU EVER]

AND I WON'T FEEL
A THING

Now that your savior is still as the grave you're
Beginning to fear me
Like cavemen fear thunder - I still have to wonder
Can you really hear me?
I bring you pain, the kind you can't suffer quietly
Fire up your brain, remind you inside you're rioting
Society is slipping
Everything's slipping away

He reaches inside his labcoat and whips out the DEATH RAY.
As he shoots beams in the air, people scatter and scream in a
panic.

> DR. HORRIBLE (CONT'D)
> *So...*
> *Go ahead - run away*
> *Say it was horrible*
> *Spread the word - tell a friend*
> *Tell them the tale*
> *Get a pic - do a blog*
> *Heroes are over with*
> *Look at him - not a word*
> *Hammer, meet nail*
>
> *Then I win - then I get*
> *Everything I ever*
> *All the cash - all the fame*
> *And social change*

People head for the exit doors. They're locked.

> DR. HORRIBLE (CONT'D)
> *Anarchy - that I run*
> *It's Doctor Horrible's turn*
> *You people all have to learn*
> *This world is going to burn*
> *Burn*

Dr. Horrible glances at a scribbling REPORTER's pad --

> DR. HORRIBLE (CONT'D)
> Actually, it's two "R"s. H, O, R, R, right.
>
> *Burn*

The big finish over, he moves back to Hammer, looking about
at the people cowering about the room.

> DR. HORRIBLE (CONT'D)
> *No sign of Penny - good.*

I would give anything not to have her see
It's gonna be bloody - head up Billy buddy

ON PENNY - she peeks out from a chair she's hidden under, recognizing the phrase she sang to Billy...

>   DR. HORRIBLE (CONT'D)
>   *There's no time for mercy*
>   (hesitating)
>   *Here goes - no mercy...*

There is an audible energy-drain as the Freeze Ray suddenly runs out of power. Doc turns, worried.

>   DR. HORRIBLE (CONT'D)
>   Thaaat's not a good sound...

He turns back and Hammer HAMMERS him right on the jaw with a punch that sends him back twenty feet, his Death Ray flying out of his hands --

ANGLE: THE DEATH RAY hits the floor and sparks and cracks. Doc stumbles up -- and Hammer is right there, kicking him back down. He finishes the last note of his song, giving Doc the finger.

>   CAPTAIN HAMMER
>   ...WAY!!!!

He kicks him again, while he's on the floor. Doc reaches for his Ray, but he's in big pain. The Captain sees -- and strolls over to grab it for himself.

>   CAPTAIN HAMMER (CONT'D)
> A Death Ray? Dr. Horrible's moving up. Let's see if this one
>   works any better than your others.

He puts a foot on Doc's chest and points the Ray down at his face. Doc sees the Ray is broken -- a little smoke pouring out the side --

                    DR. HORRIBLE
                    Don't --

                    CAPTAIN HAMMER
Give my regards to St. Peter. Or, whoever has his job, but in Hell.

He pulls the trigger.

The Ray explodes.

Captain Hammer flies back, landing in semi-conscious agony.

People duck as shrapnel from the burst weapon whizzes over them or sticks jaggedly into the walls.

ANGLE - DR. HORRIBLE

As the smoke clears, he realizes he's fine. Stands up and surveys the room.

Everyone is silent.

ANGLE - HAMMER crawls/runs whimperingly away, panicked and ashamed.

                    CAPTAIN HAMMER (CONT'D)
I'm in pain! I think this is what pain is! Mother... or someone
                        maternal...

CLOSE ON - DR. HORRIBLE as he sweeps the room, amazed. His gaze finally settles on one thing near camera.

ANGLE - PENNY

She lies in the corner, two pieces of Ray-shrapnel in her belly and chest. She is breathing shallow.

Dr. Horrible moves quickly to her, kneeling --

                    DR. HORRIBLE
                    Penny...

                    PENNY
                (breathy and weak)
            Billy... are you all right?

                    DR. HORRIBLE
            Penny no no hold on, hold on --

PENNY
It's okay. It's okay.
(trying to smile)
Captain Hammer will save us...

And she dies, eyes wide open.

MUSIC CUE -- "EVERYTHING YOU EVER"

He crouches by her body, uncomprehendingly... finally standing over her...

DR. HORRIBLE
Here lies everything
The world I wanted at my feet
My victory's complete
So hail to the king

CHORUS
Everything you ever...

DR. HORRIBLE
Arise and sing

INT. SAME – MINUTES LATER

In a classic old monster movie tableau, Dr. Horrible carries Penny's lifeless body across the room.

DR. HORRIBLE
So your world's benign
So you think justice has a voice
And we all have a choice

He brings her over to a gurney. As he gingerly places her down, two EMTs cower with fear.

DR. HORRIBLE
Well now your world is mine

CHORUS
Everything you ever...

DR. HORRIBLE
And I am fine

He watches as her body is wheeled away.

As the music continues we --

BEGIN MONTAGE:

A SERIES OF HEADLINES - "Hero's Girlfriend Murdered". "Country Mourns What's-Her-Name". "Hammer in Hiding". "Worst Villain Ever".

INT. NEWSROOM - DAY

The ANCHORS are both visibly crying. A picture of Horrible between them.

INT. BANK - DAY

Stacks of big bills are poured at his feet like Santa's mail. TILT UP to see Doc in a bank, holding a Ray. He looks fucking grim. People cower in the BG while Moist collects more money, working as Horrible's backup.

INT. THERAPIST'S OFFICE - DAY

Captain Hammer is on a couch, weeping, almost fetal, as a THERAPIST listens impassively.

EXT. STREET - DAY

The former Hammer Groupies now wear Dr. Horrible t-shirts and goggles on their foreheads, smiling at camera in the same glassy way. One of them holds up a classic fan-painting of the Doctor.

INT. DR. HORRIBLE'S LAB - NIGHT

WEBCAM VIEW IN SLO MO: Doc is in the middle of a party -- everybody dancing, FRIENDS, HOT GIRLS, Moist, Doc talking to a SUPERVILLAIN -- Doc more subdued than the people around him but smiling and holding a drink, balloons and confetti -- and the Bad Horse Chorus on the sides of frame, their smiling heads bobbing up and down.

INT. HALL/CONFERENCE ROOM – DAY

Now the music roars into the Dr. Horrible Theme as we see cutaways of Doc donning a new, cooler version of his costume.

An enormous door is opening -- a door to a conference room where wait the EVIL LEAGUE OF EVIL - seven SUPERVILLAINS and at the head of the conference table, BAD HORSE, looking majestic and expensive.

We are on the back of Doc's head as for the first time he puts his goggles over his eyes, singing --

DR. HORRIBLE
NOW THE NIGHTMARE'S REAL

--turning back to us --

DR. HORRIBLE (CONT'D)
NOW DR. HORRIBLE IS HERE
TO MAKE YOU QUAKE WITH FEAR

He enters the room and the doors shut behind him.

DR. HORRIBLE (CONT'D)
TO MAKE THE WHOLE WORLD KNEEL

CHORUS
Everything you ever...

DR. HORRIBLE
AND I WON'T FEEL

INT. DR. HORRIBLE'S LAB - DAY

WEBCAM VIEW: Doc sits, out of costume, looking at us with
pure emptiness in his eyes, finishing --

DR. HORRIBLE

BLACKOUT

A Horrible Haiku

Six days to film it

Immortalized as a dick

Then Neil stole my pants

Nathan

HORRIBLE COSTUMES
COSTUME DESIGNER
SHAWNA TRPCIC

I got an email from Joss saying, "I have a couple of projects that I'd love to see you do. One's a superhero/supervillain piece. It pays absolutely nothing at all." "That's fine!"

DR. HORRIBLE

Joss had done a quick pen and ink sketch of what he thought Dr. Horrible should look like. It was basically a man in a white doctor's blazer, like a 1950s doctor would wear, and goggles on his head. Because Neil Patrick Harris played Doogie Howser and had worn the doctor's smock and the classic doctor's look, I didn't want to do that. The costume idea boards that I had brought were from this one comic book I can't remember the name of, but it had the classic sci-fi scientist with the high mock-turtleneck. Joss loved that idea.

Fox was working with us and giving us a lot of stuff for free. Dr. Horrible's coat, because it just happened to be the same style, is the same coat that Simon Tam wore in *Firefly*, which is the same coat the scientists wore in *Alien: Resurrection*. Joss thought that was cool.

I dug through Fox stock and pulled out three or four different goggles. The ones chosen fit Neil's head right, they didn't fall off when he moved, and they had already been aged down to a certain point.

BILLY

Joss wanted that as plain-wrap as could be. He wanted basic hoodies and basic t-shirts and basic pants. Jed was at this meeting wearing a solid t-shirt and a solid hoodie, worn-out and nondescript jeans and nondescript shoes, and Joss said, "I want Billy to look like Jed." I just took a picture and created Billy's look off him.

PENNY

I basically put together Felicia Day's wardrobe without even knowing her or her style. We brought an entire rack of clothing that I pulled together with Cleo Mannell, who helped me on this show. We went to Felicia's house. What was really helpful is that Felicia's closet is color-coordinated and completely organized. So if you need the blue t-shirt for under something or you need that cute little sweater over something, it filled in certain details. We tried to use the majority of our stuff, as opposed to her own clothing, especially because of stunts – which require duplicate costumes. So we got the majority from Fox Studios and she filled in the bits. She was awesome. Felicia inspired me to do the kinds of colors I did with her, because she was the fantasy, the romance, so I tried to keep her very bright.

Below:
Nathan Fillion has a wardrobe malfunction, as Shawna Trpcic looks on.

CAPTAIN HAMMER

Joss just said he just wanted a t-shirt and pants. So I came up with cargo pants and a military boot. We worked out different kinds of gloves to find a gauntlet that he liked. The Banana Republic t-shirt, my husband Joe designed the graphic, he did a scan of his hammer – my husband's a construction worker – and he shrank it down.

MOIST

Moist was a mixture of wardrobe provided by Simon Helberg and studio wardrobe. I found some great pieces at Fox, shiny fabric jackets and things, but he also had some wonderful t-shirts. I think the pop t-shirt is his. It all blended, but yeah, we raided his closet.

BAD HORSE

At first, I thought Bad Horse was human, so I went sort of samurai, very Asian, a lot of building out the sides, almost like saddlebags. So I gave him a long braid, like a horse tail, and I tried to bring in elements that to me would say a 'dark power of the universe,' like the Horses of the Apocalypse. But I didn't think of him as a horse – I thought of him as a person who wreaked vengeance wherever he went. Once I found out it was a horse, I was sort of mortified, and I said, "Well, should I create metal costume pieces for him? Do you want feathers, or...?" Joss said, "Shawna, it's a horse. Let it go."

THE EVIL LEAGUE OF EVIL

Bad Horse's cabinet was really fun. We had Drew Goddard, who played Fake Thomas Jefferson, come to Motion Picture Costume Company, because he's six-four or six-five, and he's a forty-four extra-long. It's not like I can just get a Thomas Jefferson costume that would easily fit him! Plus, we wanted it to be authentic pieces that looked really good. So Motion Picture Costume Company put together a rack for me and we used whatever fit Drew best – we had minor alterations. Jed as Dead Bowie came to Fox Costuming. We pulled out pieces and put them on him to try to find his character, literally in the racks where we shot *Dollhouse*.

The E.L.E. from left to right: Fake Thomas Jefferson (Drew Goddard), Professor Normal (Doug Petrie), [Identity Concealed], Fury Leika (Liz Vassey), Snake Bite (Athena Demos), Dead Bowie (Jed Whedon), Tie-Die (Kate Danson).

CAPTAIN HAMMER GROUPIE T-SHIRT

Nathan Fillion was in Vegas at the time. We said, "We need a picture of you for the groupies' t-shirts." He said, "Okay, I'll send you one on my iPhone," so he took a picture of himself and emailed it to us. That's how we got the graphic for those. My husband did them all on the computer, I printed them out and ironed them on.

THE HORRIBLE EXPERIENCE

Doing a show like that where everybody's working for free, everyone tends to be more patient and more excited and more free to have fun with it. It was an incredible professional team, because we had to get this whole movie done in a few days, but I think even Joss smiled a little bit more than usual. That was one of the amazing things, and when it won the Emmy, Joss's speech summed it up: it just proves that when you do what your heart really wants, people recognize it.

(Shawna Trpcic was interviewed by Abbie Bernstein.)

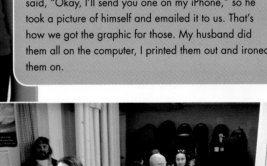

EXTRAS

Because Fox was so generous with us, we did have stock costumes, so we asked the extras playing homeless people to dress a certain way and we just had to add a jacket or a layer. We tried to control the colors, so that the fan t-shirts were the brightest people there.

Tea of Evil

DR. HORRIBLE'S TEA

HORRIBLE FANS

"All you want in life is to create something that people will dress up as," said Jed Whedon at San Diego in 2008. Job done. Within hours of Act One going up online, *Dr. Horrible* fans were making costumes and preparing amateur productions. Official merchandise soon started to appear from Quantum Mechanix, and Dark Horse Comics published a series of stories written by Zack Whedon (Christian Donaldson's cover art bottom right). As is often the case within Whedon fandom, there were charity fundraising efforts too, for example the Austin Browncoats' range of *Dr. Horrible* tea blends (above, see www.austinbrowncoats.org for more)

Left:
Want one of these Dr. Horrible Animated maquettes? Too late, all 1000 of this limited edition sold out.
Below:
The Dr. Horrible labcoat t-shirt, one of several designs produced by QMx.

DR. HORRIBLE

Top left and above:
Fans (and a cast member) at San Diego Comic-Con.
Above left:
A lucky fan models the original screen-used props at Creation Con.
Below:
Two amateur productions, from The Blue Monkey Theater Company (left) and Hockinson High School (right).

Photos courtesy Beth Nelson (opposite page, and this page center left) and The One True b!X.

San Diego COMIC-CON 2008

In July 2008, the Dr. Horrible team made an appearance at Comic-Con. Photos by Zack Whedon and The One True b!X. The quotes are taken from the panel. (It got quite rude.)

Joss: I would like to say that I directed this thing, and occasionally I told the camera where to be, but every one of these guys showed up so dialed in that I was just like, "I'm happy to be here!"

NPH to Nathan: You're still Captain Hammer!
Joss: You thought that was acting?
Nathan: It's actually shaped like a little hammer. [Outraged screams from the audience]... I mean little for a hammer... I showed Joss one time, he won't shut up about it!
Joss: It was a great day. The day he got the part of Mal!

78

Joss: Besides the fact that we all had an enormous amount of fun, this really was designed to be a model for a new way to put out media, a new form of artistic community that involves all of you guys, all of us, and maybe not so much some other people. I'm an advocate of evolution over revolution, I'm not trying to bring down the studios – I still work there, as do we all pretty much, and I'm grateful for it… but things are changing, and it's really important that as they change we make sure they're changing for the better, and *Dr. Horrible* was a little bit about that, about putting power in different hands. The wrong hands.

Questioner: Was this music something that burned deep inside your soul, or did you just come up with it…
Maurissa: Oh, it still burns…
Jed: Kinda itches…
Maurissa: We're seeing a doctor for it.

Felica: What? I forget the question… [gesturing at her lap] I'm Twittering down here… [realizes this could be misconstrued] No! I mean…
Simon: Her pants are off…
Felicia: [blushing with appalled embarrassment]: Wow. It's really hot in here!
NPH: And wet.
Felicia: [punches NPH] I'm going to keep my hands on the table now.

Joss: "Writing [my songs] was torturous joy, I think a little more torturous for me because Jed actually can play instruments and sing. It's like I get the kit, it's not painted, you have to nail it together, it's like getting home something from Ikea… it takes me way more hours than just having it. But it wasn't really until I heard them sung by these guys that I realized how much they meant to me."

Awards!

ACADEMY OF TELEVISION ARTS & SCIENCES – EMMYS

○ Outstanding Special Class – Short Format Live-Action Entertainment Programs

HUGO AWARDS

O Best Dramatic Presentation, Short Form

STREAMYS

O Audience Choice Award for Best Web Series
O Best Directing for a Comedy Web Series (Joss Whedon)
O Best Writing for a Comedy Web Series (Maurissa Tancharoen, Jed Whedon, Joss Whedon, Zack Whedon)
O Best Male Actor in a Comedy Web Series (Neil Patrick Harris)
O Best Editing (Lisa Lassek)
O Best Cinematography (Ryan Green)
O Best Original Music (Jed Whedon)

PEOPLE'S CHOICE AWARDS

O Favorite Online Sensation

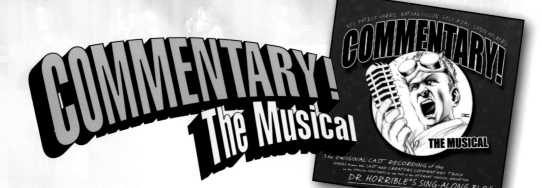

01. COMMENTARY!

Music and lyrics by Joss Whedon
Performed by the cast and writers

All:
Commentary
Commentary
Fasten your seatbelts – it's a commentary

Everyone loves these "making-of"s
The story behind the scenes
The way that we got that one cool shot
And what it all means
We'll talk about the writing
We'll probably say "It's great!"
And the acting – so exciting
Except for Nate

Nathan:
I phoned it in

All:
Commentary
Commentary
Set course for wonder – it's a commentary

Cast:
Bring back the cast, we'll have a blast
Discussing the days of yore
Moments like these sell DVDs

Writers:
We need to sell more
We've only sold four

Jed:
We'll tell you which jokes were Joss's

Zack:
Maurissa's

Maurissa:
Or Jed's

Joss:
Or Zack's

Writers:
We won't have those awkward pauses...

Neil/Maurissa:
And you'll be dazed by the haze of blazing praise
Arrays of ways to rephrase:
"Those were the days"

Neil:
Laid on so thick it'll make you sick
That's the trick to all these
Commentaries

All:
Commentary
Here comes the insight
It's a film-maker's journey
It's a road to adventure
It's a burst of fruit flavor
It's a most uncommon commentary...
Commentary!

Jed: Thanks for coming over everybody, I just know we can pull together and make this the best musical commentary ever!

Neil: You said it Jed!

Jed: Thanks Neil.

Zack: Boy, it sure better be the best ever, because we've used up an entire song and we're only halfway through the first shot.

Nathan: We're not gonna make it! We got nothin' to say, we're all gonna die!

[Slap!]
Felicia: Nathan! Get a hold of yourself. We'll be fine, we have so many fascinating insights to sing about.

Maurissa: Why don't you start Felicia?

Felicia: I don't discuss my process.

Neil: Ooh-ooh, I have a question! An Internet musical is a wacky idea that's zany, where did it come from?

Joss: It came from pain.

Jed: Uh, let's not talk to Joss.

Zack: He's sad and confusing.

Maurissa: It actually came from solidarity, does anyone remember the Writer's Strike of last year?

Everyone: Uh, um, what...

Felicia: Uh, what do the writers do?

02. STRIKE!

Music and lyrics by Joss Whedon
Performed by the writers

Newsreader: Dateline: September 2007. Things are looking grim in the negotiations between the writers and the studios. AMPTP spokesman, Nicholas Counter says, quote: "I will grind the Writers Guild into a fine paste, snort it up my nose, and cut it with baby powder and sell it to underprivileged kids" unquote.

Felicia: That's unfair!

Nathan: We've got to act

When you start negotiations
With integrity and patience
And they just cry "Battle stations!"
What's to like?
When you ask a small amount and
Then encounter Counter's counter
And the deal is tantamount to
"Take a hike"

You can't sit around with your head in the sand
You pull it out, you stand up and
You strike

When you hear their lawyers talking
Saying our behavior's shocking
It's convincing as a cockney
Dick Van Dyke
When they leave the town unstable
Then they come back to the table
And say "Now we should be able –
Kidding! Psych!"
We ask them for bread and get "Let them eat
cake"
They figure a stomach ache will break
The strike

So strike
For all the writers
Strike
For a living wage
Until these wrongs are righted
We won't write another page

Jed:
Wipe off that smile – the style is bile
And rage is all the rage

As the fall turns into winter
There appears a bunch of splinter
Groups who wonder what this Inter-
Net is like
While the tide is turning tepid
And the town is feeling trepid-
Atious time for us to step up
To the mic
We've got all these dynamite plots to use
It's time to light the fuse or lose
The strike

Joss:
And lose we did
Impressively

All:
Slunk back to our offices
Declaring victory
If you need your residual
Why did you all agree

I'm proud I walked the line
With writers, fans and friends of mine
But now I ask what was it finally about
And years from now I'll tell my tyke
Just what it feels like to strike
Out

Nathan: Say, that's a fascinating piece of

information! If you're a boring person.

Neil: I never knew a song could feel so much like a really, really long history class. Maybe it's time we heard from the actors.

Nathan: I'm an actor! Maybe I should go first.

Neil: No, I was referring to the good actors.

Nathan: Neil, why don't you step back just a second–

Neil: You know what, why don't you step up?

Zack: How about Felicia?

Felicia: I don't discuss my process Zack.

Stacy: Excuse me.

Maurissa: Er, what honey?

Stacy: I'm sorry, it's my turn.

Jed: And you are?

Stacy: Stacy.

Jed: And I would know you from?

Stacy: Groupie number two. I have a solo now.

Zack: That makes little or no sense.

Jed: Tell you what, why don't you sit in the corner over there by Steve and if we have time left over–

Stacy: Joss...

Joss: No, yeah, I think she should sing. She's young, up-and-coming. America would want to know what Tracy's–

Stacy: Stacy.

Joss: –all about. It's good for the whole team, for the family. This is about *family*.

Zack: How much did you pay him?

Stacy: Ten dollars.

Joss: I was going to share.

YOU STAND UP AND YOU STRIKE

03. TEN DOLLAR SOLO

Music by Joss Whedon and Jed Whedon
Lyrics by Joss Whedon
Performed by Stacy Shirk and Neil Patrick
Harris

Stacy
They think I'm no one
I don't have a name
But I want to live forever
Just like in "Fame"
(But not as depressing; I hear the remake is
better)
Two weeks in the business

Still got no breaks
The people all say I'll never
Have what it takes

But I can't lose
I've paid my dues

Ten dollar solo
Worth every dime
My path is so steep
But my god Joss is cheap
And doesn't mind wasting your time

See the Bad Horse chorus
Jump into frame
They tell me I'm not ready
To get in the game

But I'll show them
My ATM

Ten dollar solo
Not bad so far
There's internal rhyme
Although not every instance
And the meter is occasionally a little bit
bizarre

They say Hollywood is heartless
And only the strongest survives
But I like it plenty
I gave Joss a twenty
And got back a dream and two fives

So here comes my

Neil:
Ten dollar solo – solomente baby!

Stacy:
No, this is my scene

Neil:
Your scene, I've seen your scene

Stacy:
You're wonderful, Neil
But Joss made me a deal

Neil:
Suck it – I gave him fifteen…
yeaeeeeeaaahh!!!

Stacy and Neil:
Ten dollar lame-o

Stacy:
Are those the words now?

Stacy and Neil:
How could I (you) know
That Joss pays his debt
With this cheesy duet
When you stoop so low
Then you say so long
Solo

[Stacy runs crying from the room]

Neil: Was it something I did?

Maurissa: Yeah, let's all cry for the white girl who got a solo for no reason.

Jed: Maurissa, don't use our bedroom voices.

Zack: Joss, that song had no content. It wasn't even about the movie it was about itself, that's like breaking the ninth wall. It's pointless.

Joss: Maybe this whole thing is pointless, maybe we should just–

Nathan: You know, while you're all jibber-jabbering I'm watching the screen and do you know what I see? Not me. And this isn't the first not-me scene I've noticed.

Felicia: Oh this is the one we were supposed to do at Universal but we ran out of daylight and we stuck it in an alley. And we had Chinese food that day, but not Chinese food from Chinatown, even though we were *in* Chinatown, and it made my stomach rumbly, but the traffic covered it, and Neil was so cute and blinky and… I don't discuss my process.

Nathan: Oh I know, Neil's the star. *Cute little Neil!* Well, there's no easy way to say this, so I'm just gonna sing it…

04. BETTER THAN NEIL

Music by Jed Whedon
Lyrics by Joss Whedon and Jed Whedon
Performed by Nathan Fillion
Backing vocals by Maurissa Tancharoen
Horn arrangements by Maurissa
Tancharoen

Hey ladies
Sit down, relax
I got a story to tell…

Every night I lay awake

FALLING INTO NATHAN'S EYES IS EASY

With sorrow in my chest
I think of NPH and wonder
Is he getting rest?
Does he know each second
He's only second best?

Tossing in his bed
What's he wearing? Dread?

I'm better
Better than Neil
In so many ways
It's almost unreal
Oh sure he can sing
And piggies can squeal
It's not a big deal
I'm better

So he was out on Broadway
While I was on the soaps
Who's got the high score
On "Ninja Ropes"?
Who's got a bullet-proof
Car like the Pope's?

Look at Neil mackin'
So sad he's so lackin'

He makes seven figures
And gets Emmy nods
I make seven-layer
Bean dip of the gods
I'm also in Halo 3
What are the odds?

Now my ears are ringin'
'cause all the girls are singin'

I'm better
Better than Neil
At so many things
It's hard to conceal
Oh sure he does magic
Magic's not real
How dumb do you feel?
I'm better

Neil played a kid doctor
Well, so did I, dude
But I was much younger
And totally nude
Neil kept that white coat on
Great, doctor prude

Look there Felicia goes
Another deal you couldn't close, yeah

I wink at a woman

She needs a drink – stat!
She knows I get everything
I'm aiming at
Except for the Pope car
I lied about that

At least I'm not prone
To singing alone

Look at his smallness
Compared to my tallness
My porcelain doll-ness
My port-in-a-squallness
My Kids-in-the-Hallness
My Pink-Floyd's-"The-Wall"ness
My three parts of Gaulness
My just all-in-allness

My wonderful me-ness
My hammer – the people can tell
That I'm awfully swell
While Neil has a weird smell
I'm just saying: Purell

I'm better
Better than Neil
At – where do I start?
Romantic appeal
We both went for Penny
And who copped a feel?
The true Man of Steel
I'm better than Neil

Yeah yeah yeah
I'm better than Neil
Just jumped off a moving
Automobile
He plays with his phone
While tires they squeal
It's my scene to steal
I'm better than Neil

Neil: Nathan, are you trying to say– what are you trying to say there?

Nathan: Nothing, that's just an old sea shanty my mother used to sing to me. My pirate mother.

Neil: Oh, for a minute there it sounded like you were–

Nathan: It's a shanty.

Neil: Songs can hurt like a fist.

Nathan: Life isn't a competition, Tiny. The only question you have to ask

yourself is, "How good a Joey Buchanan was I?" A man's Buchananity is what separates him from reptiles and lawn furniture.

Zack: You know I'd like to hear from Felicia. Or any other living being on the planet.

Felicia: Well, my Internet series *The Guild* was one of the inspirations for Dr. Horr–

[groans]

Jed: Uh nobody cares about that.

Felicia: Well I mean *The Guild* is just a small part–

Jed: Seriously, el no a care-o.

Felicia: I have dozens of loyal fans. Baker's dozens. They come in thirteens.

Jed: Look at the screen, here you all are singing together. Felicia, what's going through your head?

Felicia: Art?

Jed: As in?

Felicia: Lofty art-ness. I certainly wasn't thinking about how cute Nathan is.

Nathan: Are you sure?

05. THE ART
Music and lyrics by Joss Whedon
Performed by Felicia Day

When I first meet Hammer I stumble and
stammer
'Cause that's what it says to do in the script
But whenever I would practice that was just an
act this
Is all so real – he's so well equipped
Falling into Nathan's eyes is easy
I don't even realize he's cheesy
'cause jeez he's so great
Wait

But it's not about Nate
Gotta concentrate
'Cause I'm looking for internal truth and not
a date

No it's not about Nate
'Cause it's all about the art

Perfect, mysterious, comes from above
Magic as a magic thing and lovely as love
A gift from Olympus, who send me the muse
And shoes

If I walk with a twitch in the scene in the kitchen
First date jitters aren't to blame
'Cause all Penny feels are these nine inch heels
Which are gonna make me fall and die and aren't in frame
But my death-scene pumps are really dreamy
Right when Billy dumps my corpse, it's steamy
To see me all – wait
Oh I'm sorry I lost my train of thought I'm being such a bimbo!

But it's not about shoes
Even if they're sweet
They should focus on my tragedy and not my feet
No it's not about shoes
When it's all about the art

Memory, method, primal and deep
All Stanislavsky, Strasberg and Streep
Truth, Mr. Lipton, that's how you build
The Guild

But it's not about The Guild
I'd be killed
If I shilled
For The Guild
On somebody else's time
Then again, I sort of was killed
The Guild season one available on DVD plus new episodes at watchtheguild.com we also have t-shirts

Joss:
Felicia!

Catch Guild fever

My tortured actor's process:
Stand here and do what Joss says
Remember that it's not about

The weird beard on Otto
The beer and Clamato
The hair in the cheese and
The Guild's second season
And Brand New Day Neil
That intro's unreal
A horse – not too shabby

Now steady's all crabby
The soldier boy extra
Good times – no, I'll text ya
The Red Bull Neil's drinking
I'm dead and I'm blinking
And Joss's ungluing
When I mention pooing
Which I'm always doing
I mean mentioning pooing
I mean art
Art
Art's really easy...

06. ZACK'S RAP
Music by Jed Whedon
Lyrics by Zack Whedon, Jed Whedon, and Maurissa Tancharoen
Performed by Zack Whedon
Backing vocals by Maurissa Tancharoen

I don't do songs, I'm all about the written word
And you should see me write graffiti, concrete's preferred
There's nothin' worse than hearing verse sung like a tweety bird
Unless it's screamin' 'cause I'm beatin' up a theater nerd
Or haven't you heard –
I'm the black sheep in a band of brothers
Who sit around singing showtunes
Giving back rubs to each other
You make a musical, don't matter if it's witty or pretty
That's a one-way ticket to buttkicked city
Where you all are permanent residents
Do you need a little more evidence?
Dr. Horrible – hey that sounds kinda dark and cool
Sing-Along Blog – what the f*!k is this? Preschool?

Zacky's doing us a little favor
Blessin' commentary with his flavor
Don't tell him it's a musical
'Cause then he might kill us all

You people are in freefall, straight into a cheese ball
I get a message please call my bookie buddy, he's all –
What the hell is up with you up on Hulu

Thought we were layin' low after that hooker snafu
I said, hey listen, you just misunderstood
I got to get in on this web sh#t while the gettin's good
I didn't know there were songs, that sh#t makes me sick
My brother said it's about a guy who kills some chick

Jed:
Hey, weren't you a prince in "The King and I" in seventh grade?

Zack:
No, but I was backstage in the dark getting laid

Jed:
Weren't you Pigpen in that "Charlie Brown" show we did?

Zack:
No, I just wandered on stage during my homeless period

Jed:
Didn't you sing about the business in "Annie Get Your Gun"?

Zack:
Is that what that was? I've been tanked up since ninety-one

Jed:
Weren't you the Tin Man in "The Wizard of Oz" or something?

Zack:
Yeah, but I played the f*!k out of that part

Zacky's doing us a little favor
Blessin' commentary with his flavor
Don't tell him it's a musical
'Cause then he might kill us all

I wrote all the good lines and I made them funny
But I was only in it for the horrible money
Plus some were cut out, 'cause Joss is such a wuss he
Cut my line for the girl, "The Penny is my p_ssy"
Not to mention my whole Moist storyline
Where he gets caught selling blow at a rest stop and serves time
And then he gets out and tries to get his sh#t together and teaches art to underprivileged kids at the local high school, but things take an interesting turn when an old gambling buddy comes to collect. See it's his former life coming back to haunt him. You can't outrun your past. See? Get it? That's the point, Joss. It's compelling!

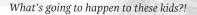

TOLD YOU HOW I F#!KED YOUR MOTHER

What's going to happen to these kids?!

Zacky's doing us a little favor
Blessin' commentary with his flavor
Don't tell him it's a musical
'Cause then he might kill us all

Simon: Hey guys, how's it goin'?

Zack: Hey Simon. What's up?

Jed: What is he doing here?

Zack: What's up?

Simon: I was just wondering if I could maybe sing my song now. I know it was technically cut out.

Zack: Yeah.

Simon: I dunno, I understand with the time slot, on the Internet, that there wasn't time. But I really have a lot of demons that I'd love to get out.

Zack: Go for it.

07. MOIST

Music and lyrics by Jed Whedon
Performed by Simon Helberg
Piano solo by Simon Helberg

Nobody wants to be moist
A bunch of overactive pores
I struggle opening doors
And I lose every tug
of war

Nobody wants to be wet
Though sweet soul I do secrete
Can't make damp fingers snap to the beat

The microphone is dripping
My baritone is slipping
A rhyme into this line I'll have to foist
Nobody wants to be moist

Nobody wants to be moist
Though on the dance floor I glide
On stairs I'm petrified
(that's how Harry Wismer died)

Nobody wants to be soaked
Though it is with a graceful ease
I deduce in which way blows the breeze

Oh sure I have the power
To make paste from a powder
But last time I did that no one rejoiced
Nobody wants to be moist

A man so ancillary
My little song is buried
Not till the commentary is it voiced
Nobody wants to be
Nobody wants to be
Nobody wants to be moist

Neil: How come Simon gets to play his own piano solo? I haven't even had a song yet.

Nathan: You always were jealous of Simon.

Neil: Jealous? Ha!

Nathan: Deny it all you want.

Neil: No no, I thought you were joking, that's just how I laugh.

Felicia: Jed, these guys are ruining the musical. Did they ever get along?

Zack: Yeah, can't we all just hug? I mean, what up bitches?

Jed: There was one thing that brought us all together, Neil, Nathan and I were like best friends that day, remember guys?

Neil: Best friends? Ha!

Jed: I thought we were friends?

Neil: No we are friends, it was a good day, that's just how I laugh.

Nathan: We really were best friends Zack.

Jed: I'm Jed.

Nathan: And you always will be...

08. NINJA ROPES

Music and lyrics by Jed Whedon
Performed by Jed Whedon, Neil Patrick Harris, and Nathan Fillion

Jed:
There's a game on my phone
That I sometimes like to play when I'm alone
Go to google, type it in
Click the extreme edition

And in moments you'll begin and you'll be thinking –
This is dope

Ninja Ropes
Ninja Ropes

Neil and Nathan:
We did not get along

Nathan:
I thought Neil was given far too many songs

Neil and Nathan:
Both threw insults at each other

Neil:
Told you how I f#!ked your mother

Neil and Nathan:
But what made us tight as brothers and forever one would hope

All:
Ninja Ropes
Ninja Ropes

Careful as you hurtle from one circle to the next
Sometimes double back to dodge the gravity vortex
Two ropes is the key to keep from wheeling way too far
Nathan holds the record –

Nathan:
One nineteen point seven yards

Jed:
Now the shoot is complete

All:
And into our separate lives we do retreat

Neil:
But instead of Solitaire

Neil and Nathan:
Sinking deep into despair

All:
It reminds us the connection that we share and helps us cope

Ninja Ropes
Ninja Ropes
Ninja Ropes...

You've got just one life to fly and dive from place to place
Don't ask why a ninja can survive in outer space
Friends say, "Hey man can I have a go?" and I say, "Nope"
Simple in its game play and yet epic in its scope

Simple in its game play and yet epic in its scope

Ninja Ropes
Ninja Ropes
Ninja Ropes...

Maurissa: Wow, a really long fake guitar solo. Aren't you guys forgetting something? Like the rest of the ensemble?

Nathan: What is an ensemble? It's just assembly spelt like, in French.

Maurissa: This was a team effort y'know. Come on in guys!

09. ALL ABOUT ME
Music and lyrics by Joss Whedon
Performed by Steve Berg, David Fury, Marti Noxon, Rob Reinis, Stacy Shirk, Maurissa Tancharoen, and Jed Whedon

Maurissa:
Here's a tale as old as time and tide
A simple girl, a wanderer
Who grew up starry-eyed

Stacy:
You see me for an instant
You see everything inside

Steve:
No matter what the movie tries to hide

Groupies:
It's all about me
It's all about me

Maurissa:
It's groupie number one

Stacy:
Groupie number two

Steve:
It's groupie number three

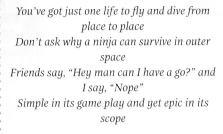

WE'VE GOT A STORY ARC AND FROTHY BEERS

Groupies:
And if I had the screen time I deserved you'd see

Maurissa:
It's all about me

Newscasters:
Here's a tale that can be told at last
Of desks that must be sat behind
And news that must be cast

Marti:
The moment is so fleeting

David:
But our talent is so vast

Newscasters:
The so-called stars are hopelessly outclassed

Marti:
It's all about me

David:
It's all about me
With all the latest breaking headlines on this tragedy

Marti:
And if I had the screen time I deserve you'd see

Newscasters:
It's all about me

Rob:
They call me moving guy
Because I move the audience to tears

Jed:
We're not just chorus boys

Bad Horse chorus:
We've got a story arc and frothy beers

Stacy:
They'll never know how much I gave
The film is locked, the door is shut

Steve:
They wouldn't give me final cut
But what you'd see

All:
Is all about me
It's all about me
It doesn't matter where I'm listed on IMDB

David:
It's last, but in the meantime I think you'll agree

David and Maurissa:
Finally

All:
It's all about

Not them
Not them
Not them...

Neil: Wow, I guess I never saw it from the perspective of people who don't matter.

Nathan: But Maurissa, you co-wrote the movie, why not just make yourself Penny instead of Monkey Face?

Felicia: I'm standing right here.

Nathan: With a face like a monkey.

Felicia: Well that's really funny if someone doesn't have a vestigial tail.

Maurissa: It's OK, I didn't want the part of Penny anyway.

Neil: Really? What do you mean?

Nathan: Yeah, tell Neil what you mean?

Neil: What *do* you mean?

Felicia: I don't look like a monkey.

Joss: What do you *mean*?

10. NOBODY'S ASIAN IN THE MOVIES
Music and lyrics by Maurissa Tancharoen and Jed Whedon
Performed by Maurissa Tancharoen

I wrote all Penny's lines and her song, you know
I even sang her part up on the demo
But when it's time to cast the show
Did they want somebody yellow – hell no

Nobody's Asian in the movies
Nobody's Asian on TV
If there is a part there for us
It's the groupie in the chorus
That's me
I begged and I pleaded please don't pass me by
They say, hey give us a hand
Go stand in the back with that fat guy
My role, though be it brief, at least
It isn't Viet Cong, it's comic relief

Nobody's Asian in the movies
Nobody's Asian on TV
If there is a part there for us
It's a ninja, a physician
Or a goofy mathematician
Or a groupie in the chorus
That's me

Who do they want before they want an Asian?
A Mexican
Who do they want before they want an Asian?
A Black
Who do they want before they want an Asian?
A Persian, or a Cajun, or an Indian
Or an American-Indian played by a Mexican
Or if you're lucky someone Asian
Like me

Jed:
But Maurissa, movies couldn't even be made without Asians.
We need them to play the parts we're not willing to.

Maurissa:
You're right, Jed!

Without the Asians in the movies
Without the Asians on TV
Who'd play the goofy mathematician
The computer technician
A wise old healer from Japan
A short but wealthy businessman
Sell Korean groceries
Do your laundry thank you, prrease
We're the victims of a crime
We'll be loving you long time
If your movie is a bore just
Watch the groupie in the chorus
That's me

Maurissa:
I guess my parents will be proud of me after all.

Jed:
What does your dad do again?

Maurissa:
Oh! He's a nerdy, funny scientist.

Jed: Isn't your dad a Transpo guy?

Felicia: Oh like an Asian could do that.

Maurissa: I'm gonna go in the corner and play my violin and… math.

Joss: I tried to warn you, the truth never helps anyone.

Jed: Joss don't start.

Joss: I didn't start this.

Jed: Then don't do the middle.

11. HEART, BROKEN
Music and lyrics by Joss Whedon
Performed by Joss Whedon

A caveman painted on a cave
It was a bison, was a fave
The other cave-people would rave –
They didn't ask "Why?"
Why paint a bison if it's dead
When did you choose the color red
What was the process in your head
He told their story
What came before he didn't show
We're not supposed to

Homer's Odyssey was swell
A bunch of guys that went through hell
He told the tale but didn't tell
The audience why
He didn't say, here's what it means
And here's a few deleted scenes
Charybdis tested well with teens
He's not the story
He's just a door we open if
Our lives need lifting

But now we pick pick
Pick pick pick it apart
Open it up to find the
Tick tick tick of a heart
A heart, broken

It's broken by the endless loads
Of making-ofs and mobisodes
The tie-ins, prequels, games and codes
The audience buys
The narrative dies
Stretched and torn

Hey, spoiler warning:

We're gonna pick pick
Pick pick pick it apart
Open it up to find the
Tick tick tick of a heart
A heart, broken

Jed:
Joss, why do you rail against the biz
You know that's just the way it is
You're making everybody miz

Zack:
These out-of-date philosophies
Are for the dinner table, please
We have to sell some dvds

Jed, Maurissa, Zack:
Without these things you spit upon
You'd find your fame and fanbase gone

Maurissa:
You'd be ignored at Comic-Con

Joss:
I sang some things I didn't mean
Okay, let's talk about this scene
I think it's great how Ryan Green –
Oh this is no good
I thought J-mo would back my play
Now Zack and they all say

We're gonna pick pick
Pick pick pick you apart
Open you up and stop the
Tick tick tick of a heart

A heart…

Joss: Goodbye.

Jed: Great, good, everybody out. I'm not producing a commentary with crappy commentators!

[Everyone leaves, except…]

Neil: Guys?

12. NEIL'S TURN
Music and lyrics by Joss Whedon
Performed by Neil Patrick Harris

Have they all gone?
Yes! It's Neil's turn
No more writers to whine

Now the whole show is mine

No more Nathan
With his bean dip
Say goodnight, Frankenstein
'Cause it's my turn to shine

I can do all of their jobs
I can just play with these knobs
And I'll sound fine

It's a one-man
Like Hal Holbrook
Like that showcase for Liza
It's "Neil with an I"

Hey Felicia
You were great, kid
But you just had to die
'Cause there's no "team" in "I"

I'll sing my own harmonies
I'll go as low as I please
Or I'll go high

Welcome everybody to my commentary
I've got so much talent it's a little scary
Is my every random thought insightful – very
Not just entertaining; I'm a luminary

I'll charm the chicks
Are those things real? Ha!
Do magic tricks
Was it the three of clubs? Ho!
Lay down some tap
And I can rap

My name is Neil and I'm here to say…

No I can't rap
That was painful
Let's move on to the part
Where I talk about art

Look at that shot
We used cameras
There's a boom guy in frame
He was great – what's his name?

What was his name?
What should I say?
The choices are endless
And here I am at last, alone, and friendless
No I'm not friendless
I've got some friends
They'll be here when this ends
If this ends
What do I say

What does this switch do – it turns out the lights
Now it's dark and I'm lost and alone
And what's with all these chords?
What's with all these weird chords?
Somebody help
Somebody say cut
Somebody say action
Somebody say something
I'm so afraid
Somebody say cut
I'm so alone…

Felicia: Neil?

Neil: Felicia?

Felicia: You're not alone. You're just kind of a douche.

Jed: We're here with you Neil.

Nathan: Even me!

Joss: And we've resolved all our problems!

Neil: Just like that? I thought you were–

Zack: We only have three seconds left, everybody be happy.

Everyone: Yay!

13. COMMENTARY (REPRISE)
Music and lyrics by Joss Whedon
Performed by cast and writers
Ooo's and ahh's by Maurissa Tancharoen and Jed Whedon

All:
Hope you had fun
'Cause now we're done
You've listened to every word
Seeing it through
Makes each of you
A huge f#!king nerd

But you're unfazed
By the maze of craze malaise
The lazy phrasing betrays
How well this pays
So here's a toast
To who suffered most
While we coasted through this

Neil:
Commentary!

All:
Commentary
Here's the big finish
Where we build up the tension
And we get really quiet
Then we stop being quiet
And repeat the title – commentary

Neil:
Depressing shot

14. STEVE'S SONG
Music by Jed Whedon
Lyrics by Jed Whedon and Joss Whedon
Performed by Steve Berg

I'm still a bit suspicious why they asked me to be in this
And, yes, my best guess is my s's
My friends would never consciously
Exploit somebody's weakness
They say my voice possesses a sweetness
Jed texted me, said "Commentary's coming,
Steve would you please grace us with a song"
I heard the dulcet tones his hands were strumming
I knew it's not this lisp
It's been my talents all along

Steve's song
A showcase of my skills
Steve's song
Alive are these hills
With Steve's song
Steve's song
Yes yes yes yes

Maurissa scoffed at my suggestion –
Hammer needs a few more sweaters
I still think six vests sounds much better
But now I'm super nervous
Since I'm standing in the studio
Like Phil Collins singing Sussudio
Su-su-su-su-sussudio

And yes on the horizon there's a sequel
With some substantial bits for mister me
It's evidence they see me as an equal
I'm not groupie number seventy six thousand
six hundred and six point seven six two three
five niner squared – I'm three

Steve's song
A maestro on the rise
Steve's song
A nice pleasant surprise
Is Steve's song
Steve's song
Steve's song
Steve's song
Steve's song
Yes yes yes…

No.

HAMMER NEEDS A FEW MORE SWEATERS

AFTERWORD BY
NEIL PATRICK HARRIS

I have to say, on reflection, that *Dr. Horrible* is the single best thing that I've ever done. I look back at all of the chapters in my professional life, and they were either long and rambling, or had major ups and downs. But from start to finish, *Dr. Horrible's Sing-Along Blog* was nearly perfect.

I had just arrived into New York City when I got the initial call from Joss. I remember it well – sitting in a yellow cab, crossing the Triborough Bridge, looking at the amazing landscape of Manhattan, and Joss Whedon is on my phone, seeing if I'd 'be interested' in starring in a super villain movie that he wanted to produce and direct. A musical, no less. I think I said yes maybe a dozen times before we hung up, just to make sure he heard me.

Receiving the initial email with a link to Billy/Horrible's songs was a treat. I downloaded them immediately, and had my iPod on a constant loop for weeks. Jed sang my part. Though, I'll bet if you ask him, he'd say it was the other way around.

Recording the music was surreal. It all happened at the then Whedon residence, upstairs in a room they had built for just this sort of creative, musical happenstance. I was sequestered to a soundproofed, glass-encased recording studio, and Jed handled the mixing and computering and such. Maurissa was there. Joss wandered here and there, muttering his preferences. We did all of the songs back-to-back, saving the growlier, rockier stuff for the end of the day, when my voice was most damaged. Everyone seemed pleased, and I was anxious to hear the finished product. (Products..? Songs..? Canon..?) I was anxious to start to learn the lip-sync. (Lip syncs..? Moving on...)

Everyone at my local Equinox gym must have thought I was a psychopath for about two weeks there, when I was trying to get the 'mouthing' down perfectly. I'd put one song on repeat, and practice it for hours, usually while running on a treadmill or doing sit ups. I find memorizing at the gym is helpful, not sure why. Concentration? Anyway, point being, I looked like a boob.

The first day of filming was memorable. I arrived on set, got in my costume, had make-up applied and my hair gelled, then went to the corner of a parking lot and got pulled up into the air by my underpants. Repeatedly. I think I smiled through the humiliation. I'm relatively optimistic that those were tears of joy...

We powered through each day, a guerilla unit, grabbing whatever shots we could, improvising set ups, perfecting stunts, rehearsing dialogue. It's weird – as a whole, it whizzed by, but when I think back to specific scenes, I can recount almost every detail. Rehearsing the 'closing of the dryers' moment of 'Freeze Ray' with Felicia, watching Simon get sprayed down with water before every take, and marveling at how often Nathan complained about the size of his trailer. Watching stuntwomen get hurled into trash, Bad Horse chilling by a conference table, Mustached-Jed being held prone by two grips as he was thrust sideways into frame, Nathan berating the caterer for their lack of jerky. I'll remember it all forever.

Months later, Joss called Felicia, Nathan and me to his then *Dollhouse* offices for our initial screening. We all three sat in the darkness, mouths agape, as we watched what we had created. We were overwhelmed and giddy, wanting to watch it again. It was at that moment I really felt like this was not only something special, but a true 'once in a lifetime'. I couldn't wait to see the general public's reaction. To read the forums after Part One and see where everyone thought it was going. To read them after Part Two and see how everyone thought it would end. The almost uniform approval from the online community was fantastic. When the server shut down due to overuse, I knew that we had won. That it was a success.

Dr. Horrible was, in every way, a passion play. From initial concept through the final credit, everyone gave from their hearts to create something both massive and intimate, global and personal. We were all on strike, and hungry to work. Joss wanted to prove that content could be created on the creators' terms, and still turn a profit. I wanted to take the part as written, and really make it sing (see what I did there?). I've probably watched it thirty or forty times now, and listened to both soundtracks hundreds more. I'm a true fan, and it still blows my mind that I'm one of its stars. I'm a lucky man, indeed.

Thanks for reading, and thanks for digging Dr. H –

N

HORRIBLE. HAMMER. HI-DEF.
You can almost smell Bad Horse.

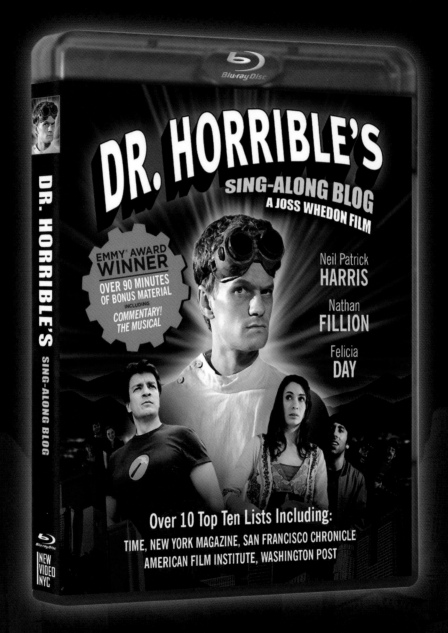

THE SHEET MUSIC

HORRIBLE THEME

Music by Jed Whedon

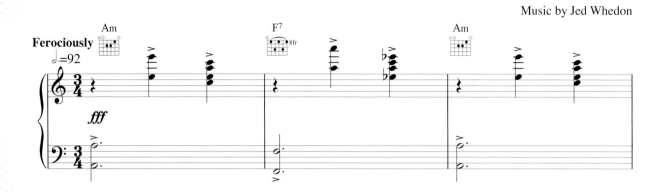

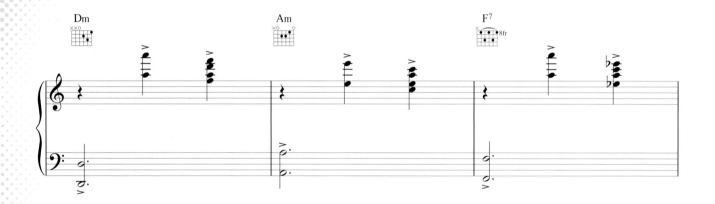

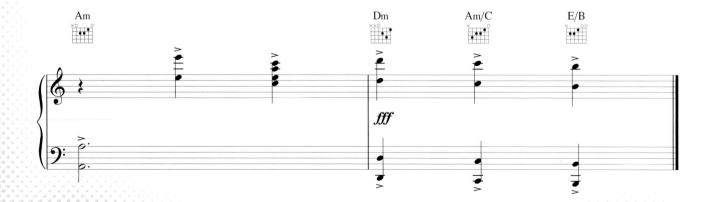

MY FREEZE RAY

Brightly
♩ = 144

Music and Lyrics by Joss Whedon

1.Laun - dry day   See you there
2.Tell you how   How you make

Un - der things   Tum - b - ling____   Wan - na say
Make me feel   What's the phrase?   Like a fool

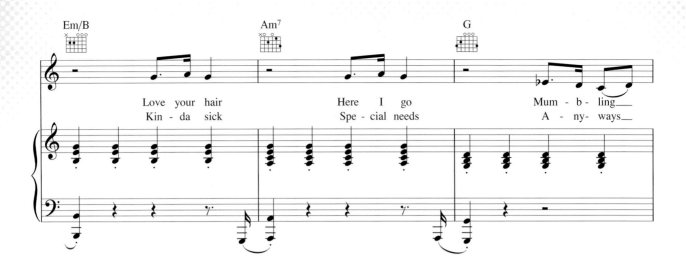

Love your hair
Kin - da sick

Here I go
Spe - cial needs

Mum - b - ling
A - ny- ways

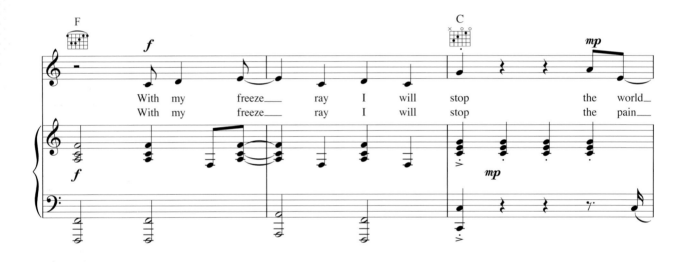

With my freeze ray I will stop the world
With my freeze ray I will stop the pain

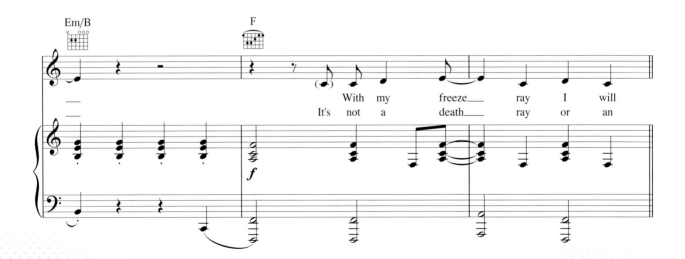

With my freeze ray I will
It's not a death ray or an

1. find the time_ to find the words to

2. ice beam that's all John-ny Snow_ I just think you need

time to know that I'm___ the guy___ to make___ it real___ The feel-ings you don't dare_

___ to feel I'll bend the world___ to our will And we'll make time_____ stand

still_____

That's the plan   Rule the world   You and me   A - ny day_

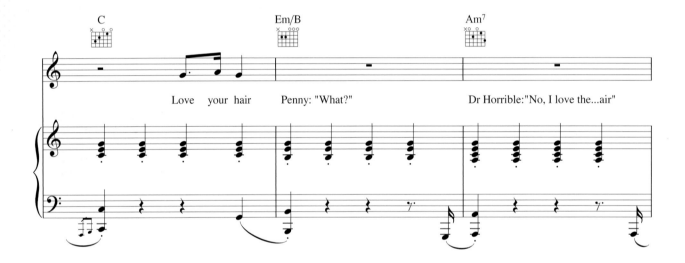

Love   your hair   Penny: "What?"   Dr Horrible: "No, I love the...air"

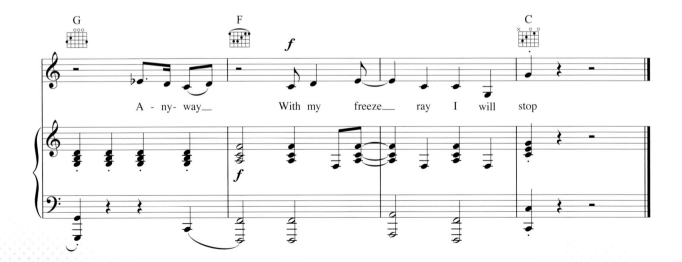

A - ny- way_   With my   freeze_ ray   I will   stop

Music by Jed Whedon and Joss Whedon
Lyrics by Joss Whedon

CARING HANDS

Music by Jed Whedon
Lyrics by Maurissa Tancharoen and Jed Whedon

Will you lend a ca-ring hand to shel-ter those who need it? On-ly have to sign your name don't

e-ven have to read it. Would you help? (Spoken) "No? How about you?"

Music and Lyrics by Jed Whedon

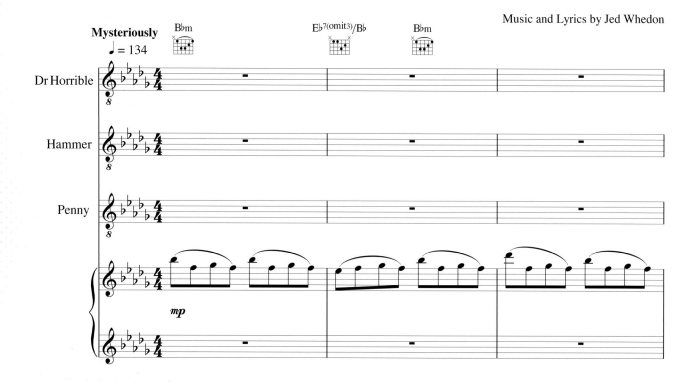

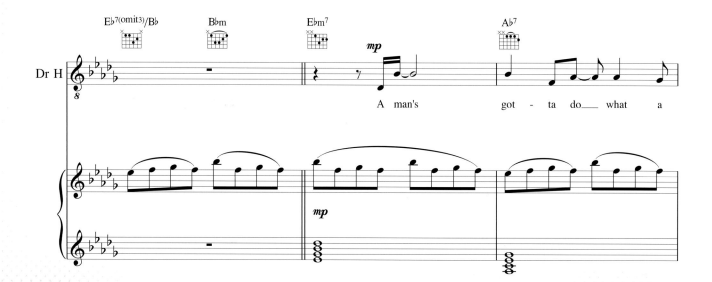

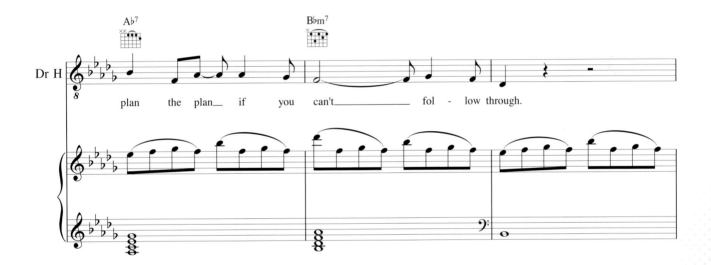

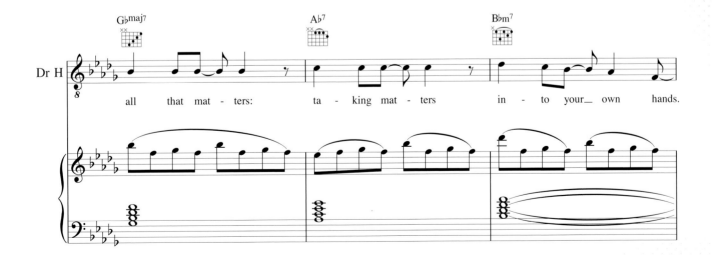

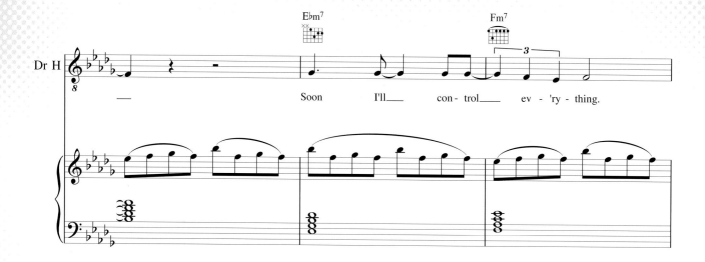

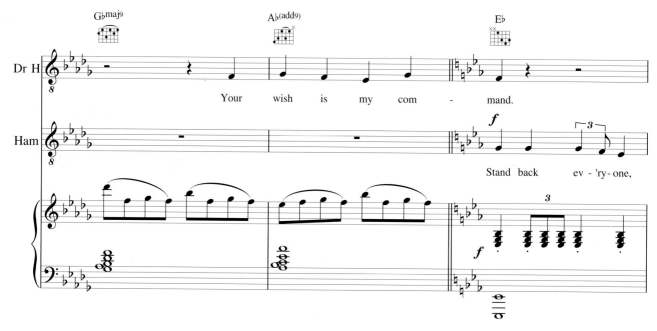

Cap - tain Ham - mer's here, hair blow-ing in the breeze. The day needs my sa - ving ex - per-

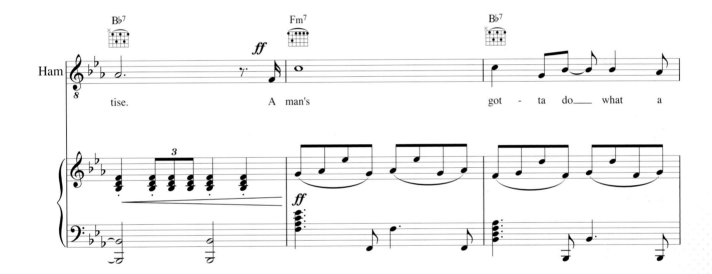

tise. A man's got - ta do what a

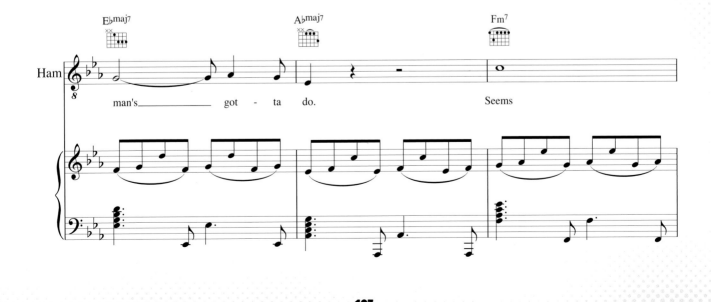

man's got - ta do. Seems

des - ti - ny___ ends with me_____ sa - ving you. The

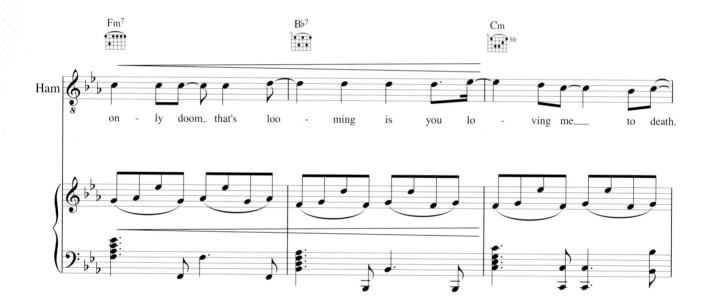

on - ly doom_ that's loo - ming is you lo - ving me___ to death. The

So I'll give you___ a sec___ to catch_ your_____

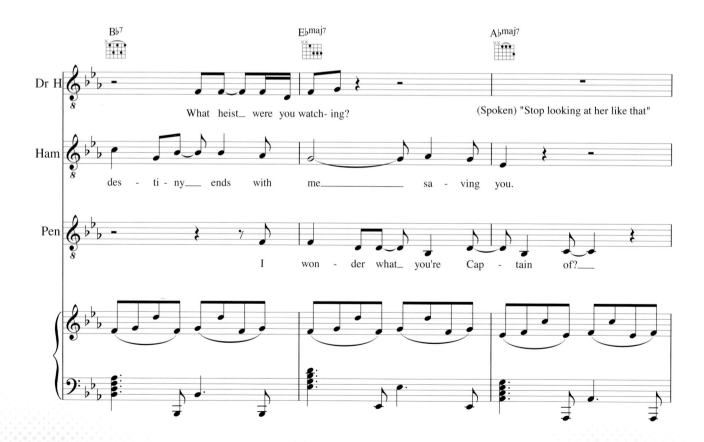

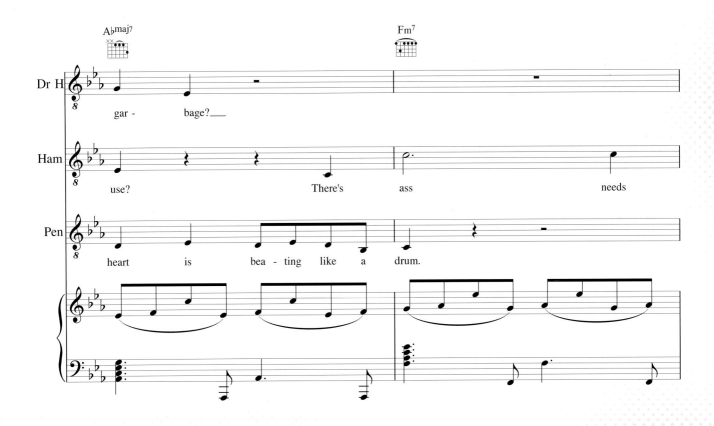

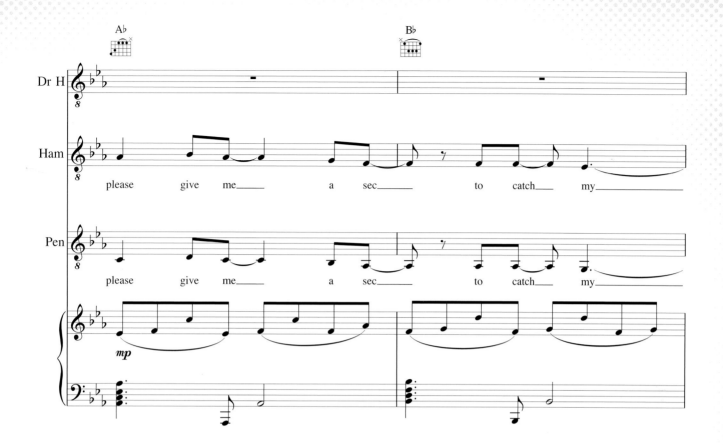

please give me___ a sec___ to catch___ my___

please give me___ a sec___ to catch___ my___

___ breath.___

___ breath.___

(Spoken)

Balls.

MY EYES

Music by Jed Whedon
Lyrics by Maurissa Tancharoen,
Joss Whedon and Jed Whedon

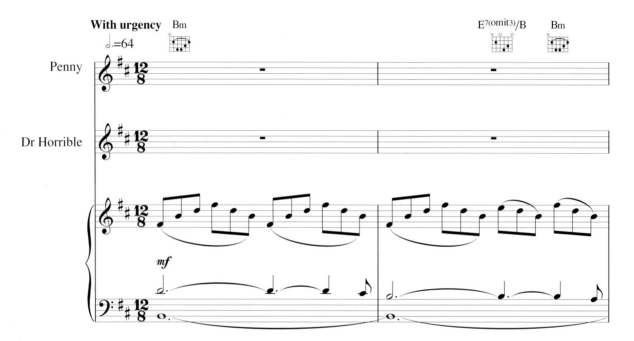

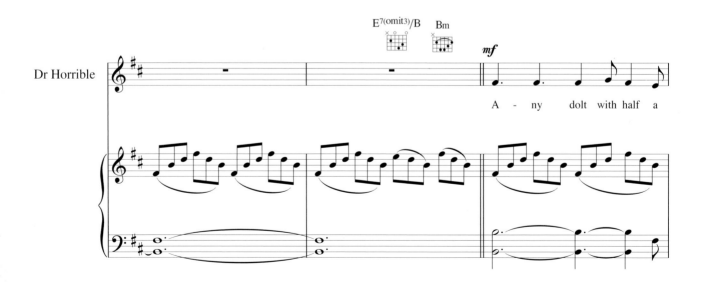

A - ny dolt with half a

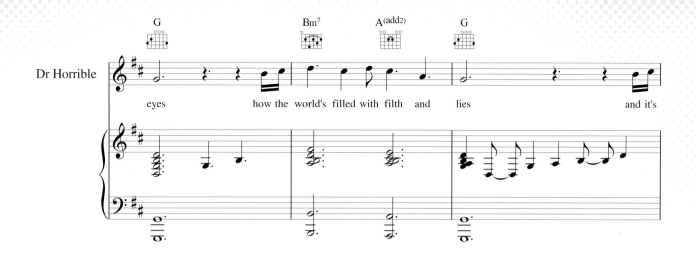

Dr Horrible: eyes how the world's filled with filth and lies and it's

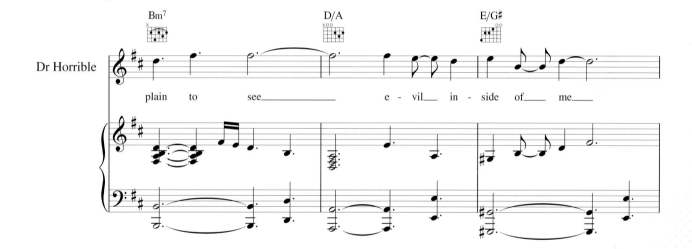

Dr Horrible: plain to see_____ e - vil__ in - side of__ me_____

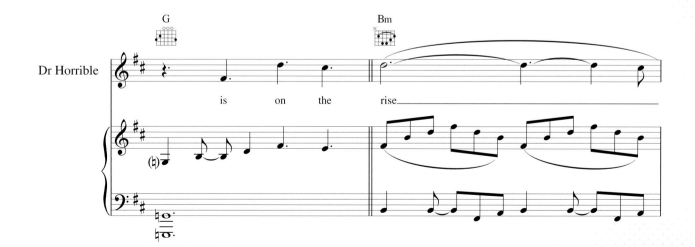

Dr Horrible: is on the rise_____

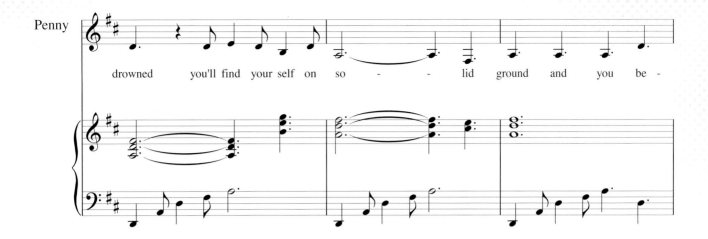

drowned you'll find your self on so - - lid ground and you be -

lieve there's good___ in ev-'ry-bo-dy's heart Keep it safe and

sound._____ With hope, you can do your part to

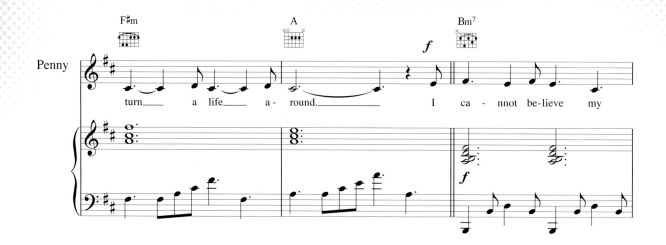

turn____ a life____ a - round._____ I ca - nnot be-lieve my

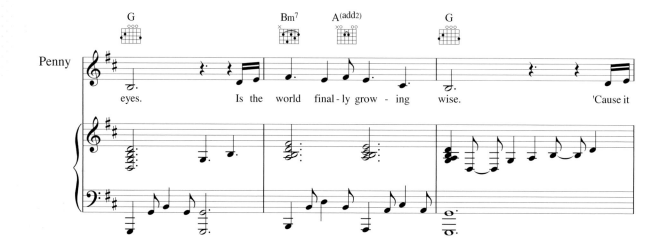

eyes. Is the world final - ly grow - ing wise. 'Cause it

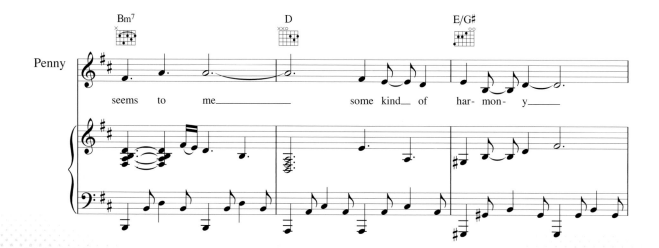

seems to me_____ some kind__ of har - mon - y____

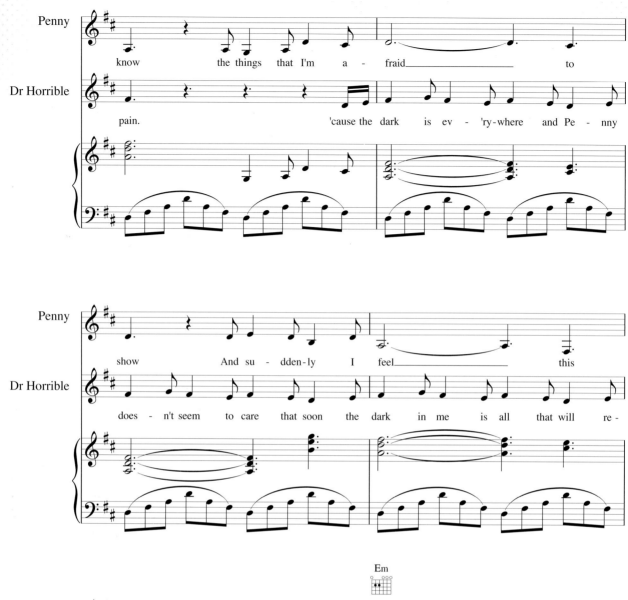

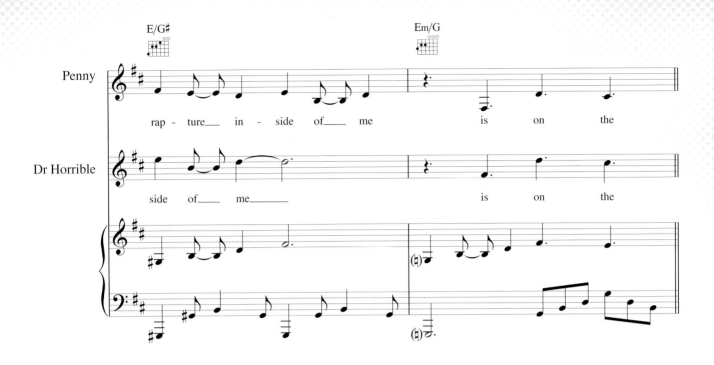

Music by Jed Whedon and Joss Whedon
Lyrics by Joss Whedon

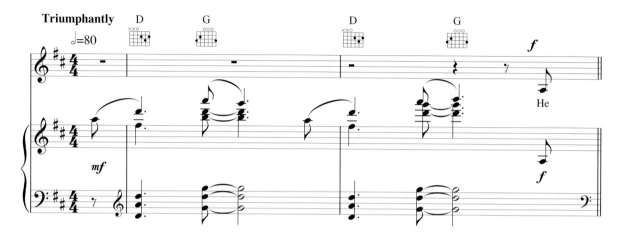

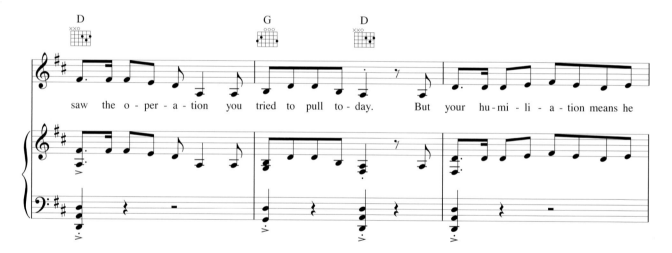

126

way.   There will be blood, it might be yours, so go kill some-one. Signed:Bad Horse.

PENNY'S SONG

Music by Jed Whedon
Lyrics by Maurissa Tancharoen and Jed Whedon

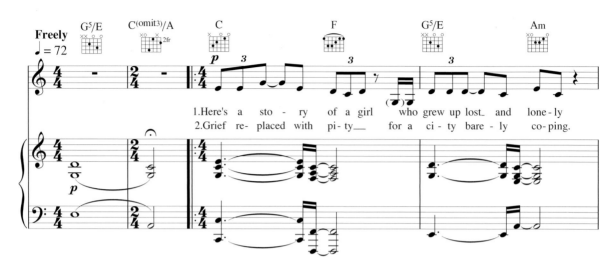

1. Here's a sto-ry of a girl who grew up lost_ and lone-ly
2. Grief re-placed with pi-ty_ for a ci-ty bare-ly co-ping.

Think-ing love_ was fai-ry-tale and trou-ble was_ made on-ly for me.
Dreams are ea-sy to a-chieve if hope is all_ I'm ho-ping to be.

More movement

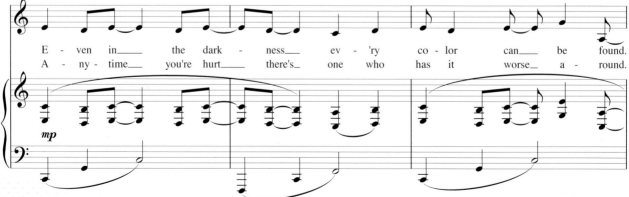

E-ven in_ the dark-ness_ ev-'ry co-lor can_ be found.
A-ny-time_ you're hurt_ there's one who has it worse_ a-round.

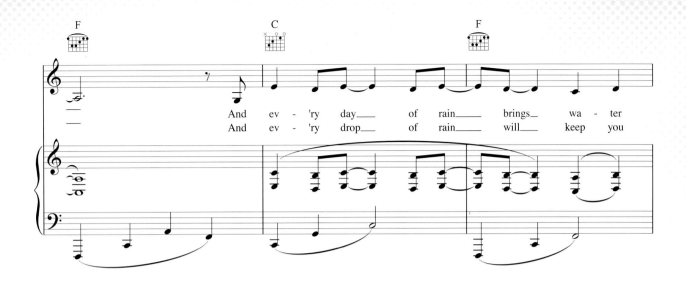

And ev-'ry day____ of rain____ brings wa - ter
And ev-'ry drop____ of rain____ will____ keep you

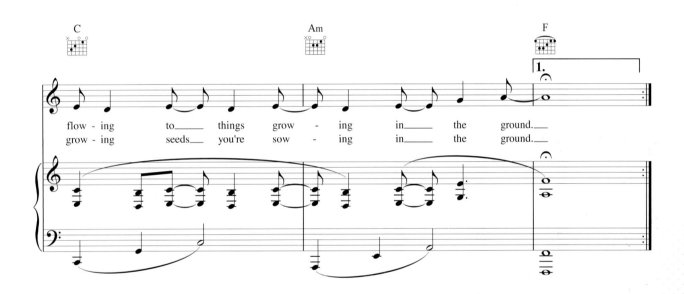

flow - ing to____ things grow - ing in____ the ground.____
grow - ing seeds____ you're sow - ing in____ the ground.____

1.

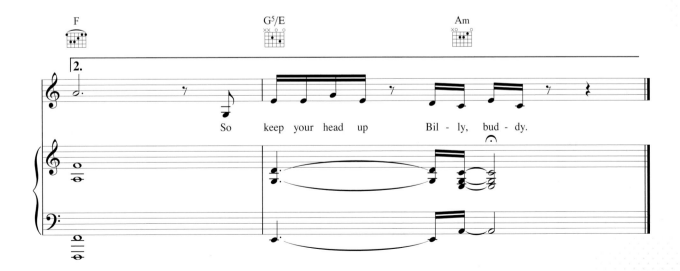

2.

So keep your head up Bil - ly, bud - dy.

BRAND NEW DAY

Music by Jed Whedon and Joss Whedon
Lyrics by Joss Whedon

1. This ap-peared as a mo-ral di-lem-ma 'cause at
2. All the times that you beat me un-con-sious I for

first it was weird thought I swore to e-li-mi nate the worst of the plague that de-vour-ed hu-man-i-ty it's
give all the crimes -in-com-plete-lis-ten, hon-est-ly I'll live, Mi-ster Cool, Mi-ster Right, Mi-ster Know-it-all is

true   I was vague on the "how" so how can it be that you   have shown me the light?_____   It's a
through. Now the   fu-ture's so bright and   I   owe it all to

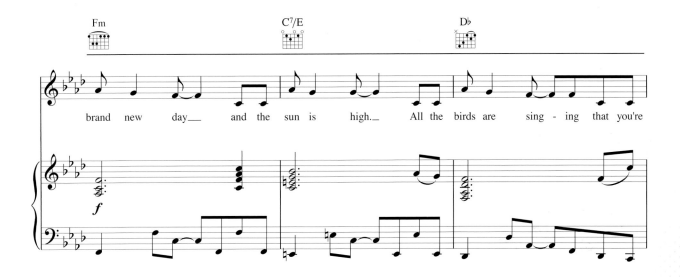

brand   new   day___   and the   sun   is   high.__   All   the   birds   are   sing - ing   that   you're

gon-na die.   How   I   hes - i - ta - ted   now   I   won-der   why?   It's   a   brand   new   day.__

you, who showed me the light._____ It's a

brand new me,___ I got no re - morse Now the wa-ter's ri - sing, but I know the course. I'm gon-na

shock the world, gon-na show Bad Horse it's a brand new day.___ And Pen-ny will see___ the e -

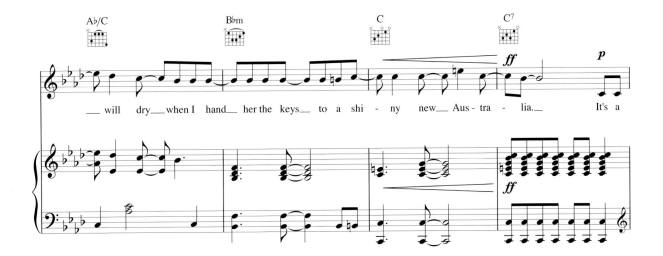

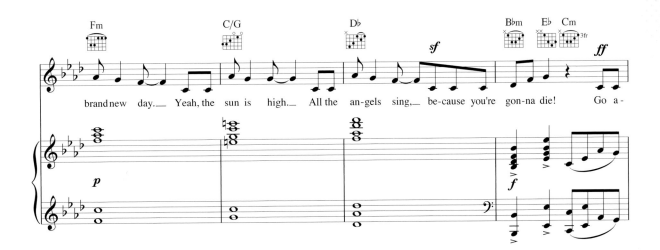

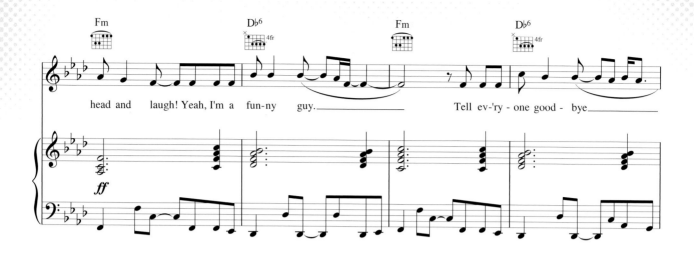

head and   laugh! Yeah, I'm a fun-ny   guy._____   Tell ev-'ry-one good-bye_____

It's a brand new   day.___

SO THEY SAY

Music by Jed Whedon and Joss Whedon
Lyrics by Joss Whedon

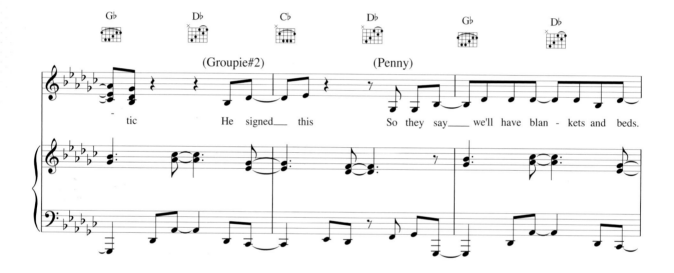

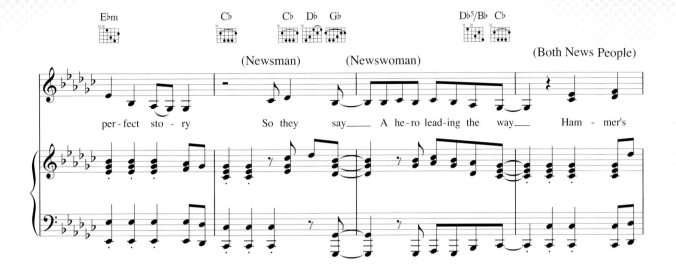

per - fect for__ me.   So they   say.__ I guess it's pret-ty o - k__   A - fter

years of storm - y   sail - ing have__ I final - ly found the bay.__

(Penny) There's no

(Dr Horrible) There's no

(Repeat to fade)

EVERYONE'S A HERO

Music and Lyrics by Joss Whedon

It may not feel too clas-sy Beg-ging just to eat but you know who does that? Las-sie. And she

al-ways gets a treat. So you won-der what your part is 'cause you're home-less and de-pressed. But

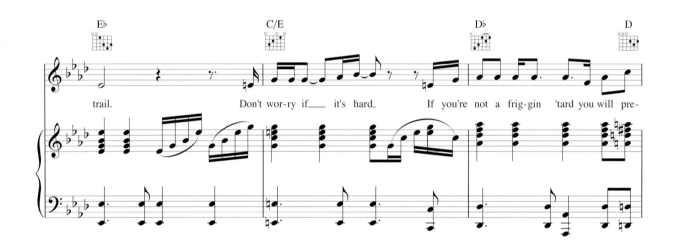

SLIPPING

Music and Lyrics by Joss Whedon

1. Look at these peo-ple a - ma - zing how sheep will show up for the slaugh ter
2. Now that your sa - vior is still as the grave you're be - gin - ning to fear me. Like

No - one con-dem-ming you line up like lem-mings you led to the wa - ter.
cave-men fear thun-der - I still have to won-der can you real - ly hear me?

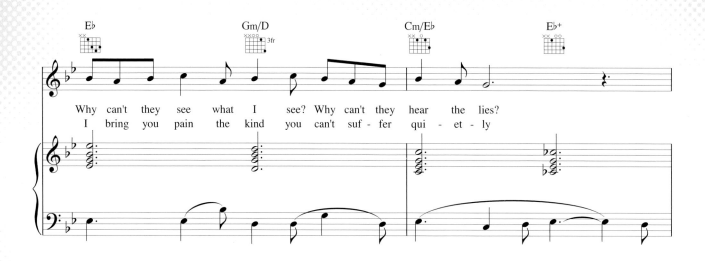

Why can't they see what I see? Why can't they hear the lies?
I bring you pain the kind you can't suf - fer qui - et - ly

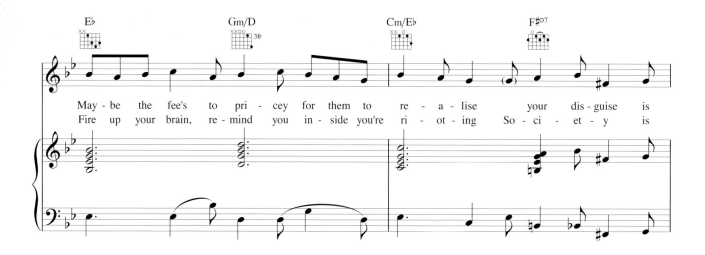

May - be the fee's to pri - cey for them to re - a - lise your dis - guise is
Fire up your brain, re - mind you in - side you're ri - ot - ing So - ci - et - y is

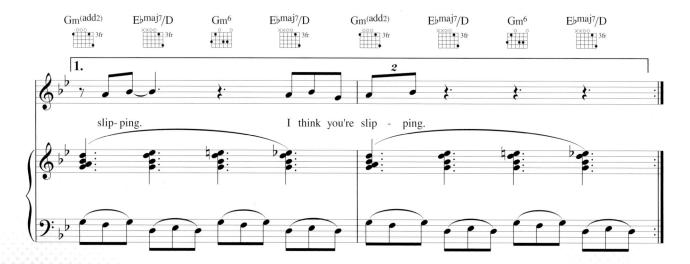

slip - ping. I think you're slip - ping.

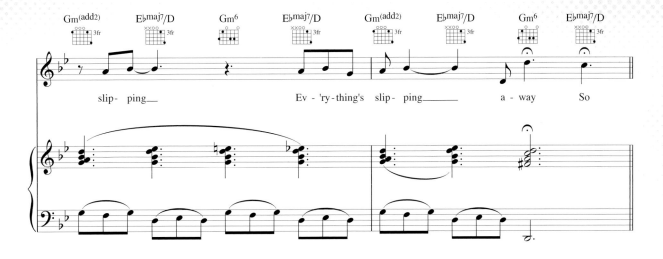

slip- ping___ Ev - 'ry-thing's slip- ping_____ a - way So

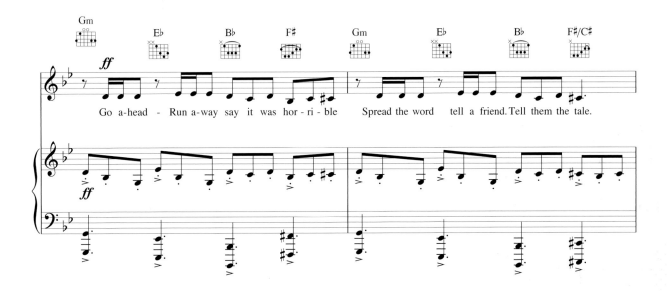

Go a-head - Run a-way say it was hor - ri - ble Spread the word tell a friend. Tell them the tale.

Get a pic do a blog. Her-oes are o - ver with. Look at him, not a word. Ham-mer, meet nail.

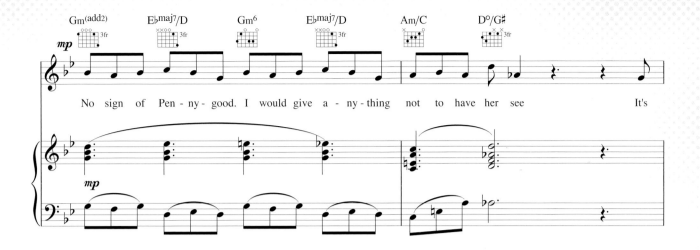

No sign of Pen-ny-good. I would give a-ny-thing not to have her see It's

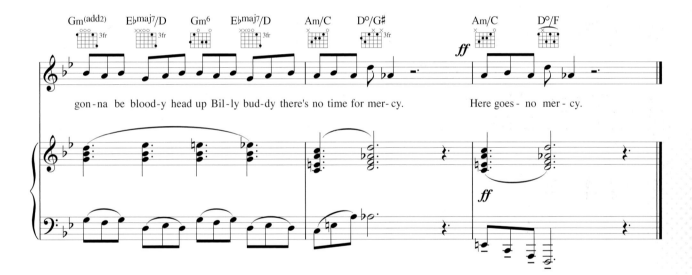

gon-na be blood-y head up Bil-ly bud-dy there's no time for mer-cy.   Here goes- no mer-cy.

Music and Lyrics by Joss Whedon
Bridge by Jed Whedon

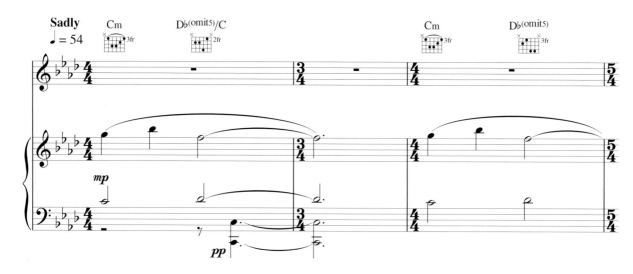

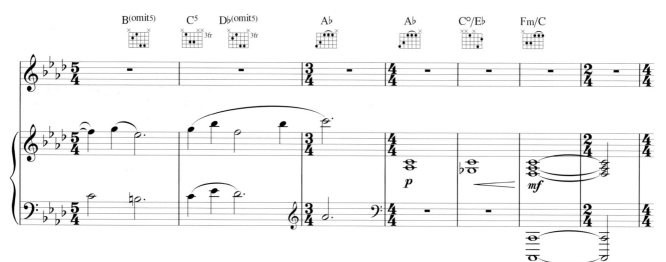

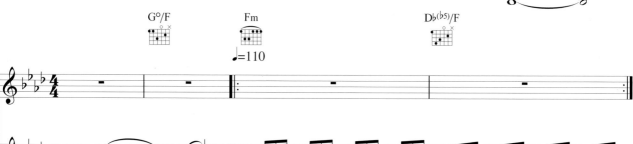

1.Here lies ev - 'ry - thing.
2.So your world's be - nign.___

The world I wan - ted at my feet. My
So you think jus - tice has a voice. And

vic - to - ry's___ com - plete,___ So hail___ to___ the king.
we all have___ a choice___ Well now your world___ is mine.

(Ev - - - 'ry - thing___ you e - - ver.)
(Ev - 'ry thing___ you e - ver.)

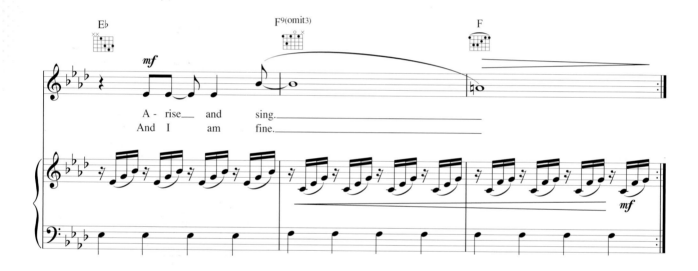

A - rise___ and sing._____
And I am fine._____

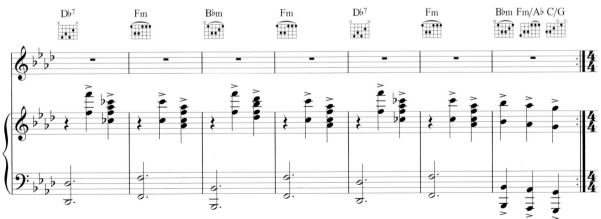

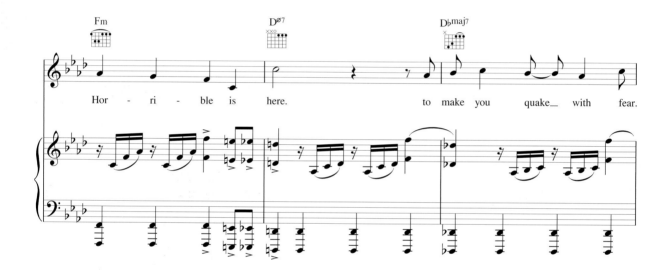

(Ev - 'ry - thing___ you e - ver)

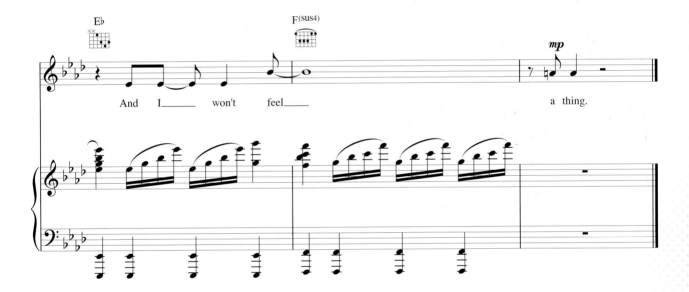

And I___ won't feel___ a thing.

Music by Jed Whedon

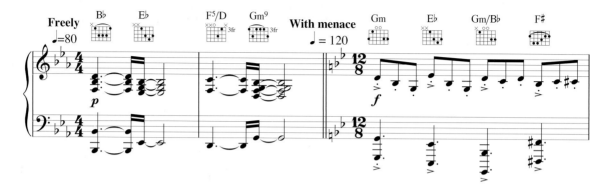

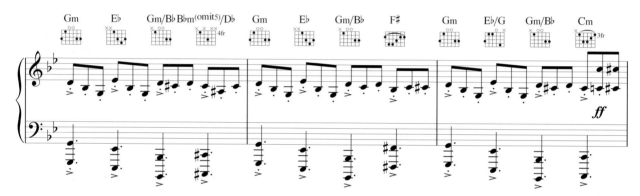

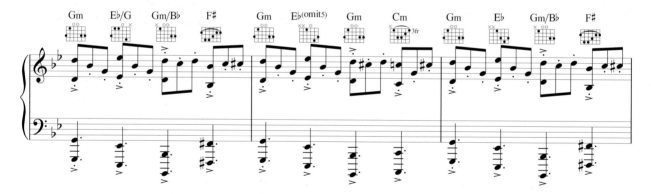

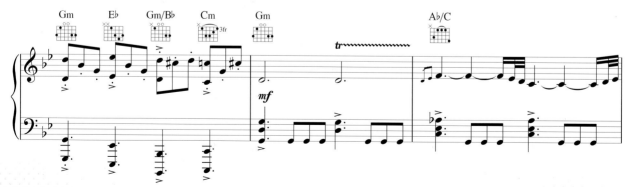

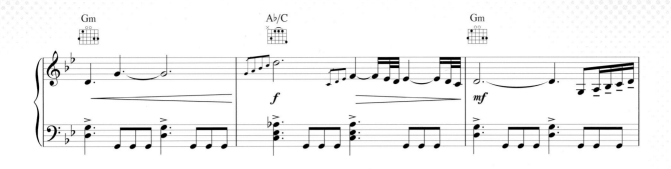

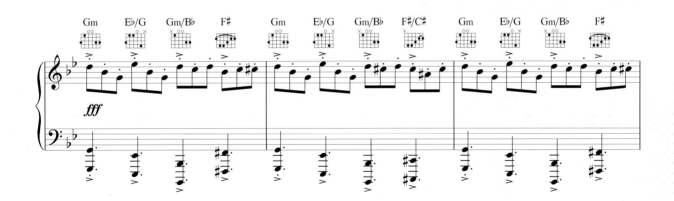

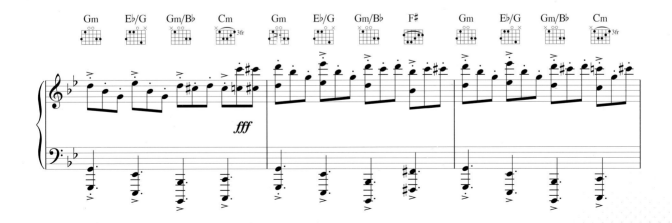

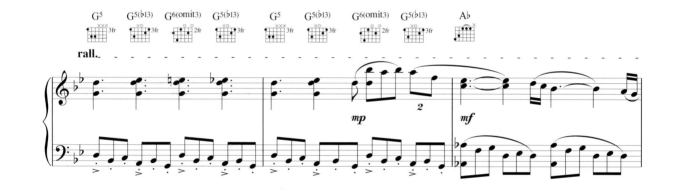

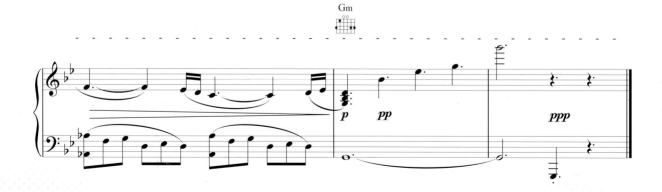